Raise cash – have fun

Raise cash – have fun

Christine Fagg

Imaginative ideas for fêtes, bazaars, social functions and all kinds of money-making entertainment

Elek Books Limited
2 All Saints Street London N1

© Christine Fagg 1969

Published by
ELEK BOOKS LIMITED
2 All Saints Street London N1

361.7
FA

and simultaneously in Canada by
THE RYERSON PRESS
299 Queen Street West Toronto 2B

Made and Printed in Great Britain by
Unwin Brothers Limited
Woking and London

This book is for
CAROLE
who told me to write it

Contents

Introduction — 1

1 Planning and organising an event — 5

2 Fêtes and bazaars with a difference — 18
Bon marché
St. Patrick's bazaar
Caledonian market
All the fun of the fair
Ye Olde Englishe fayre
Stars and Stripes
Continental bazaar

3 Indoor functions — 28
Hallow-e'en
St. Andrew's party
Valentine dance
Old time music hall
New-style coffee mornings
Night in gay Paree
Bridge drive
Sausage sizzle, or tramps' supper
Astrological diversion
Beauty demonstration
Cheese and wine party

4 Outdoor functions — 37
Strawberries and cream tea
Madeira morning
Sponsored walk
Safari party
Market stall
Treasure hunt
Brunch party
Carnival
Decorated floats
Stomp and sheep roast

viii   Contents

5   Seasonal fund raising — 48
Spring:
House and garden gala
Easter frolic
Hat and hair-style parade
Mad Hatters' ball
Champagne fashion show
Autumn:
Michaelmas mart and hobbies fair
Holiday memories
Evening book sale
Christmas:
Toy fair
Christmas grotto
Yuletide bonanza bazaar

6   How children can raise money — 62
Putting on a pantomime
Tots-to-teens fashion show
Carol singing
Lollipop fair
Individual efforts

7   What to make, sell and sew — 70
Methods for collecting money and merchandise
Talents project
Jumble and how to sort it
Stalls
Display and staging of goods
Easy articles to make and sew

8   Sideshows, contests and other attractions — 83
Sideshows:
Treasure hunt
China smashing
Bucket ball
Skittles
Hoopla laundry
Ringing the bottle

Light the candles
Candle snuffing
Darts with a difference
Cover the silver pieces
Electric bell ringer
Knock off the hat
Catch a fish
Contests:
Beauty contest
Baby show
Dog show, etc.
Guessing competitions
Other attractions:
Tombola
Handkerchief tombola, with lucky numbers
Hydrogen balloons
Pony rides
Pneumatic drill
Trampoline
Fried chips
Portrait sketches
Entertainments:
Dancing
Music
Physical education and sport
Services
Exhibitions
Theatrical

9 How national charities raise money   93
Annual subscription
Legacies
Covenants
Flag days
Collecting boxes, etc.

In conclusion   98

Appendix of useful names and addresses   101

Index   105

List of illustrations

1	A sponsorship form for an organised walk	40
2	A quoit tennis court	43
3	A gold turreted castle	57
4	A Christmas calendar	60
5	A simple method for erecting a frame over a stall	73
6	A banner	74
7	Book markers	75
8	A giant pin cushion	76
9	A Christmas table centre	78
10	Decorative Christmas crackers	79
11	A bath puff	80

Acknowledgements

I would like to thank all those people who have helped with criticism and suggestions.

Introduction

This is a book about fund raising. It is written for ordinary people like you and me who have reached a point in their lives where they feel a genuine desire to devote some of their time to helping others. This happens to most of us and I firmly believe that raising money can be an adventure, offering a splendid opportunity for enriching the lives of all those who are generous, sympathetic and energetic enough to take the plunge. At the same time, the reward of new friends and fresh interests will broaden your outlook and give purpose and vitality to your life.

Despite the astronomical growth of the social services in our Welfare State, there still exists a tremendous demand for money for every conceivable cause. From the local Youth Club or Friends of the Hospital, to National Societies like Cancer Research or the British Red Cross, hard cash is required to bring forth vital projects.

The book is not concerned with the high-powered methods of big business charities who employ staff to organise flag days, door-to-door collections and covenants, although I hope some of my suggestions will be of interest to them. Nobody would deny that the enormous sums raised by these organisations are magnificent achievements, but voluntary fund raising means a great deal more than just collecting money. There will always be the need for small groups of people to draw together, inspired by a single purpose and stimulated by goodwill to help others in their own practical way. It is mainly for these men and women who wish to run enterprising money-making projects for their own community that I have compiled this book.

Many of the suggestions for the functions described have stemmed from my own personal experiences in this field. Some of the ideas are not new, but I have tried to present the events with a fresh slant or a new approach. They are the result of sleepless nights spent racking my brains for ways in which to catch the imagination of the public and arouse their interest. How to make the ordinary appear dramatic and exciting and to create the spark of enthusiasm which will give a touch of magic to an ordinary, everyday fund raising effort.

To housebound mothers and those tied to ageing parents especially, this type of work provides an opportunity to reach out beyond the confines of domesticity to give whatever time they can reasonably spare from their home duties. Some people will feel compelled through personal tragedy to support a particular charity. Others will sympathise and for many different reasons will come forward, urged by some particular motive to help those less fortunate than themselves.

Be very sure that the cause you decide to support is one for which you feel concern and have a genuine desire to help. You may prefer to offer your services to a large organisation such as Oxfam, or perhaps join one of your local political parties rather than help restore the Parish Church, or assist other smaller efforts to do good in your own community. Of course, in many areas, money may be collected specifically for the local branches of National Charities such as the Spastics Society or the Cheshire Homes. Readers who would like more details on the work of charitable societies can find the complete list in *The Charities Digest* in a public library. Ask to see the list of organisations in your district. This will include addresses of the local bodies and the branch organisers of nation-wide charities. Write to the secretary of any association which appeals to you and ask for information about their work and activities. The Citizen's Advice Bureau (address from post offices) is willing to give advice about local needs and opportunities for voluntary work if you should be in doubt about where to offer your services. Study the literature carefully and when you have made up your mind – write or telephone and discuss your interest in joining. You will almost certainly receive a warm welcome and an invitation to come along and meet the chairman. Once you have taken this step, be prepared to work hard and give time and energy to the cause, but don't undertake more than you can reasonably fit into your own domestic or business obligations.

At first you will only be asked to help in a relatively minor way at fund raising events. Washing up at the coffee morning, knitting bedsocks for the Christmas bazaar or topping and tailing gooseberries for a summer sale. Gradually you will find yourself taking on more responsibility, perhaps running a stall, organising a fête, decorating a float or planning a social. This book is written in order to make your job an easier and happier one.

In the first chapter, I have explained the organisation of a committee and the general planning of all events. The following four chapters are devoted to Fêtes and Bazaars with a Difference, Indoor and Outdoor Functions and Seasonal Fund raising. Chapter 6 offers ways in which children can raise money and Chapter 7 gives ideas for things to make and sell. Chapter 8 suggests sideshows, contests and other popular attractions and in the last chapter you will find information on the methods of fund raising used by the large National Charities. Finally there is an Appendix of useful names and addresses.

I hope that this book will offer help and guidance in a practical and imaginative way to all those concerned with the stimulating and challenging task of raising money. Whether the function is large or small, held in a village, hamlet, town or suburb, indoors or out, you will find something in the following pages to increase its chances of success.

Chapter 1

Planning and organising an event

So let's make a start. We will assume you have been asked to run an annual summer fête to raise money for the local hospital. The same rules, however, will apply with slight adjustments to the organisation of most functions held to benefit charity. The first and most vital consideration in every case is advance planning. For a really large affair, a year ahead is not too soon, while for the average summer fête, bazaar or sale, six months is a reasonable time to allow for the preparations.

Before deciding on the type of event and the entertainments to provide, bear in mind the sort of locality in which you live. Do not provide a sophisticated mannequin parade or a way-out beat group if you live deep in rural Suffolk and know that the majority of the population is simple, earthy and home-loving. Alternatively, although urban town dwellers will appreciate country-fresh produce, don't expect them to rave over a display of dancing round the maypole. Try to gauge the mentality of your public and gear the sales and entertainment to suit their mode of living. Experience of other successful functions in your area will give you a guide.

Having decided this matter of policy, your first task will be to appoint a committee of willing and conscientious helpers. These will probably be drawn from members of your organisation who have, if possible, proved themselves at previous events and can be relied upon to serve faithfully. Other sources of help can perhaps be found among your friends, relations or neighbours. Think back to the past and remember anybody who may have shown interest in your charity when you mentioned it to them; now is the time to telephone or write a letter asking them if they would assist you in running this function. If they are willing to join your committee, offer a date and time to meet at your house to discuss the plans.

All sorts of people can work happily together for a worthwhile cause. You will enjoy the sense of comradeship, of pulling to-

6 Planning and organising an event

gether as a team and perhaps getting to understand someone else's way of life. Of course, there will be disagreements and difficulties to be smoothed out. We all know about Mrs. Price-Millar and how she is sure to upset poor Miss Plunket from the sweetshop. It's bound to happen and not only in your community either. But make no mistake – somebody must over-rule and make the decisions sometimes. If this is going to be you, try to develop the knack of getting the best out of people without seeming to push them around.

The committee
Ideally a chairman needs to find six people to serve on her committee, but naturally this will depend on the size of the function.

1. *A secretary* who will deal with all correspondence and keep the records.
2. *A treasurer* who will take care of the funds and who has, preferably, had experience in handling financial matters.
3. *A publicity officer* to contact the local press, organise the posters and see that the event blazons the minds and hearts of every man, woman and child in the district.
4. *A refreshments and catering official.* This is a key post and it needs somebody tough to man the tea urns and fortify the customers with plenty of sustenance against flagging spirits. She must decide how to delegate her responsibilities and her best plan will be to persuade as many individual members as possible to bake cakes, scones and pastries at home and deliver them on the morning of the fête. Those with more time to spare can help with sandwich cutting during the morning and serving and washing-up at the actual event.
5. *A stalls and competition organiser* to plan both these important features and find other helpers to run them. Ideas for articles to make and sell, amusing competitions and unusual attractions to draw the crowds, can be found in Chapters 7 and 8.
6. *A special helper* who is artistic and imaginative and as strong as a horse, who will step in where needed, concentrate on building up a decorative theme and generally assist the chairman and committee in any way she can.

The date

Choosing a date is far from easy. First it must be a convenient day for all your committee and helpers. If the function is to be held out of doors, consider the usual pattern of weather in your district at that time of the year. What other events take place in your community at that time? One way to ensure that you do not clash with the town's carnival or some other big affair is to visit your local newspaper office and look up the copies issued for the corresponding dates of the previous year and see what functions took place then. Ring up each organiser concerned (whose name is usually mentioned in the write-up) and ask him what date he has in mind for fund raising events during the coming year. Even so, it is more than likely that you will be up against some competition, especially if it's held in June or July. Determine from the beginning that yours will be the most attractive, well-publicised and popular entertainment of them all.

The place

Where you hold your fête must be planned with the greatest care. Try to borrow a field from a friendly farmer sympathetic to the cause, or a large garden from one of your members. The gardens of grand country houses also make wonderful settings for charity functions, and are often a great draw in themselves. If the event is to be held in connection with your Church, school or hospital their grounds are an obvious choice. Otherwise choose a site which is well known, easy to find or very central. Think of all the places in your community where similar events have been held in the past. Contact the owners and find out if they are willing to lend or hire for a small fee. Remember that you will need space for car parking (you can charge for this), cloakroom facilities fairly close, and if possible to be near a bus stop.

Advertising

One of the greatest reasons for an unsuccessful function is lack of advertising. Discuss how much money you can afford to put aside for this and if necessary hold a coffee morning to collect for this specific purpose. (Coffee mornings are described in Chapter 3.) Find out first if one of your members is connected in any way

8 Planning and organising an event

with a printing firm and if so, write asking him if he would consider doing your posters at a reduced price for the benefit of the charity in question. Alternatively, look up the names of printers in your local classified telephone directory and write a similar letter to several on the list and choose the least expensive.

A good sized poster is 20 × 15 inches because it doesn't take up too much space in shop windows. The cheapest and most eye-catching are printed in large, bold, black letters on a yellow background giving only the vital facts.

What it is.
A SUMMER FETE.

When it is to be held.
SATURDAY, JUNE 20TH, 1970. 2.30 P.M.

Where it is to take place.
BUTT'S CLOSE, ST. MARY'S SQUARE, BRAMFORD.

Why?
IN AID OF THE BRAMFORD HOSPITAL CHILDREN'S WARD.

Who is going to open the fete? . . .

Display, attractions or entertainments by . . .

Place an order for gummed strips for sticking on car windows, giving the same information, and consider paying your local bus company a reasonable sum for carrying them on all their transport. Approach your nearest cinema manager and ask him if he would show a slide advertising the event during the interval. Get your committee to persuade their shopkeepers to display posters and ask the Clerk of the Council Offices for permission to paste them by the bus stop, in the town square or at other strategic positions.

Another source of publicity is your local press. Place an advertisement in the 'What's On' column for several weeks before your fête – as large and bold as you can afford to make it. Contact the Editor after arranging this and ask him if he would give your efforts a write-up just before the actual day. This could be accompanied by a picture of the celebrity who is to open your fête, or an account of the attractions with special reference to anything unusual taking place. This will attract the public's attention and should make a big difference to the numbers who come along.

It may also be necessary, if the size and nature of your event warrants it, to have some programmes or programme leaflets printed, giving details of the times of the various entertainments and competitions. Advertising space can be sold to local shops and businesses to help defray the cost. The programmes can take the form of admission tickets sold at the gate on the day and in advance by members of the committee.

These instructions for advertising apply mainly to large events which are worth the expense of a printer's bill. Smaller functions can be made known to the public by creating home-made posters from large sheets of strong paper, obtainable from stationers or art shops. Paint information in bold, bright poster colours. *Making Posters* by Vernon Mills, published by Studio Vista (10s. 6d.), and other similar books available through your library, will help members with imaginative ideas to make a strong impact on passers-by.

Another method of claiming the public's attention, is by holding a parade in the town and district just before the event is held. This can be the usual loudspeaker van, giving repeated announcements of the facts, or a decorated vehicle providing a sensational tableau or scene depicting the forthcoming attractions. (This requires police approval.) A simpler form of advertisement is merely to dress up and promenade through the streets carrying sandwich boards or notices. To lure customers to a jumble sale, I saw a large pram in our market square, crammed with an assortment of weird garments and objects, pushed by a couple dressed in Victorian clothes and bearing the irresistible message, 'Come to our Jumble Jungle at 2 p.m. this afternoon at St. Andrew's Church Hall'. These, and other similar gimmicks will make a surprising difference to the numbers who turn up and support your function.

A personality

It is advisable at a very early stage to think about finding a suitable personality to open your fête. Who you will ask depends very much on whether there are any famous people living in your

10 Planning and organising an event

district. If you cast about and study your local papers, you may discover that there is a television actor, a minor film star, a model or an author living within a twenty mile radius of your home. You may even boast an explorer home from his travels, or a notable character of some kind who has gained publicity for something he or she has achieved in the not-too-distant past. If your memory and research provide nobody, you may care to ask one of the following people, some of whom will almost certainly reside in or near your town or village.

First on the list must come royalty. It does not matter how distant the connection may be. Royalty *is* royalty and this probably unassuming character is just the blessing and fillip your fête needs. Don't feel that he or she will be too grand to bother about opening your small event. Supporting worthwhile efforts for the good of the community is their job, and nobody will do it better.

Secondly, you can approach one of the Gentry. Top of the list come the titled landowners who still manage to live in their large country houses and keep up an impressive façade of gracious living. Lower down this scale come others such as the squire of the village, or the very rich prominent businessman. He may well have come up the hard way, but he's got money to burn and will probably spend freely at your stalls afterwards.

Finally there are those people who serve your town such as:

The Member of Parliament.
The Mayor.
The Medical Officer of Health.
The Chief of Police.
The Dean, Canon or Clergyman.
The Matron of the Hospital.
The Headmaster of the Grammar School or College of Further Education.

When you have decided whom to ask to open your fête, look up the correct form of written address (unless it's plain Mr., Mrs. or Miss) in a copy of *Titles and Forms of Address. A Guide to their Correct Use*, which you will find in the reference room of public libraries. The letter could be written along these lines:

The Bramford League of Hospital Friends,
42, Smitherton Road,
BRAMFORD,
Rutlandshire.

January 12th, 1970.

Dear Lord Lightbody,

You will be interested to know that the Bramford Branch of the League of Hospital Friends is planning to hold a Summer Fête on Saturday, June 20th, 1970. We hope to raise enough money to provide for the building of a day room extension to the children's ward of the Bramford General Hospital.

On behalf of the committee, I am writing to ask if you would be kind enough to come along and open the fête for us at 3 p.m. on the afternoon of June 20th. It is to be held at Butt's Close, St. Mary's Square, Bramford.

Should you be able to undertake this task for us, we shall be very honoured and most grateful. We all feel that this project for the sick children of Bramford is a very worthy one and will be deeply appreciated by the community, both now and in the future.

We hope that, despite your many commitments, you will find time to say a few words and give us your support on this occasion.

Yours sincerely,

Emma Pertwee,
Secretary.

When he replies in the affirmative, write again, thanking him appropriately and mention that you will be in touch with him a week or so before the event to make final arrangements. Ask permission also to use his name on the posters advertising the fête. On the day it is held, remember to detail somebody to meet him at the gate and escort and accompany him all the time he is present.

12 Planning and organising an event

Unfortunately, it is more than likely that several letters will have to be written before you manage to find somebody willing to perform this task for you. I have a friend with considerable nerve who solves the problem by picking up the 'phone and asking whomever she would like to come along and grace her functions. In her time, an eminent Head of State, a renowned footballer and many illustrious, radiant film stars have graciously condescended to attend her events. If you are brave enough, I can thoroughly recommend this practice as it brings incredibly satisfactory results. I need hardly add that her money-raising efforts are always more successful and twice as much fun as anybody else's. But just in case your famous personality lets you down, it is a wise move to ask a kind-hearted vicar's wife or school-master if they would be prepared to understudy and step in if necessary.

Other matters should also be considered at this early stage:

Procuring merchandise and prizes

In Chapter 7 I have given a comprehensive list of suggestions for items to make and sell at fêtes, bazaars and sales. But every efficient organiser should plan a special campaign to collect as many gifts and donations as possible before the event.

Detail each member of the committee (including yourself) to make a list of personal friends, relations, neighbours and others interested in the cause. Write or ask each person on that list if they will donate a gift or money towards the function. Members can also ask the managers of the shops and stores where they buy regularly, as well as manufacturers and bosses of big enterprises who operate in the area. Look in the local town directory and watch the newspapers, to see what goes on in your district and follow up any names which look profitable. The amount of money you finally collect will be in direct relation to the efforts made in this way in advance. You will be amazed at the response these requests will bring, but don't be disheartened at the occasional refusal or sharp word of criticism.

Here is an example of a letter which could be sent to a business man, asking for a donation of money or a prize for a raffle:

Planning and organising an event 13

> The Bramford League of Hospital Friends,
> 42, Smitherton Road,
> BRAMFORD,
> Rutlandshire.
> January 12th, 1970.

Dear Mr. Oglethorpe,

The Bramford Branch of the League of Hospital Friends is holding a summer fête on Saturday, June 20th, 1970, at Butt's Close, St. Mary's Square, Bramford. We are hoping to collect sufficient money to pay for building an extension to the children's ward of the Bramford General Hospital.

On behalf of the Chairman and Committee, I am writing to ask if you would be kind enough to present one of the household articles you manufacture to be raffled at this function. If you are unable to do this, would you be generous enough to send us a donation instead?

I do hope you will feel able to support us in this Cause, which we feel will greatly benefit the sick children of this town. We also hope that you and your family will come along to the fête and spend an enjoyable afternoon.

> Yours sincerely,
> Emma Pertwee,
> Secretary.

Police regulations

Unfortunately, there are many rules and regulations connected with running a public event and if I were to explain them all, this would be a very dull book indeed. You will be well advised to inform your local police about holding a function of any size likely to cause congestion on the roads, and if in doubt about any further points of law connected with fund raising events, do not hesitate to ask their advice. You will find them courteous, helpful and willing to stretch the law as far as it is humanly possible according to the particular circumstances, providing they are convinced of the genuine nature of the charity.

Some of the following items will arise in connection with a large number of public events and you would be wise to investigate from the appropriate authority to find out whether or not you are breaking the law.

14 Planning and organising an event

A raffle
This form of lottery is a very big and popular fund raiser, but there are various conditions which must be met, depending on the size and method of the promotion of the raffle.

In the first place, a draw or lottery is legal if the tickets are sold during the function or entertainment and winners' names are announced at the time the event is being held. The whole proceeds of the entertainment must be given to charity apart from permitted deductions for expenses actually incurred. Money prizes are not allowed and only the expense of prizes and tickets may be taken out of the profit. There is a limit of £10 which may be spent on prizes.

The regulations governing other types of raffle are more complex and it is essential to read the full details which can be found in *Voluntary Organisations and the Law relating to Lotteries and Gaming* (3s. plus 6d. postage) from

The National Council of Social Service,
26 Bedford Square, London, W.C.1.

Licensing laws
If you intend to provide intoxicating liquor at any public function, contact a publican, a caterer, or anybody else who is in possession of a full Justices' Licence. If he is willing to undertake the arrangements for supplying and serving alcoholic drinks for you, he must apply to the local Clerk to the Justices for what is called an Occasional Licence.

There is a great work called *Halsbury's Law of England*, which can be found in the reference room of public libraries. In Volume 22 full details concerning the granting of Occasional Licences are set out clearly.

Playing of music
If music is to be performed live The Performing Right Society must be contacted and asked for permission, which they may consider giving free for charity performances:

The Performing Right Society, Ltd.,
29 Berners Street, London, W.1.

If such music is played on gramophone records, it is also necessary to seek the approval of the Phonographic Performance, Ltd. Full details of the occasion must be sent in order to decide whether the fees can be waived:

Phonographic Performance Ltd.,
62 Oxford Street, London, W.1.

The Performing Right Society is not concerned with the performance of non-musical plays or sketches. In these circumstances, fees for copyright must be paid to the author. The address of the author's agent is usually given in the copy of the play. If it is not there, write to the copyright department of the publishing house and ask where to send the fees.

Control of traffic
Notify the police of the date, time and place of any function likely to involve traffic congestion. If one of your committee is a member of the Automobile Association, they will give half price reduction on signposts directing traffic for all recognised registered charitable organisations. They must be approached in plenty of time and have to obtain the agreement of police and highway authorities, which may not be granted. Full current prices are £5 5s. 0d. for ten signs, or £1 10s. 0d. for further batches of 5 or less.

Public liability
When running a function it is important to realise that you may be liable for certain accidents occurring to the general public as well as for replacement of borrowed equipment which may be damaged. Where advertisements are erected across the public highway, one must insure against injury caused by their falling on passers-by. Enquire from local insurance agents or write to

The Eagle Star Insurance Company,
1 Threadneedle Street, London, E.C.2.

Hiring a marquee
These are costly items and only worth the price for large functions. Names and addresses of the nearest firms can be found in the

16 Planning and organising an event

local classified telephone directories. Barns, outhouses and garages, if available, can be used instead to great advantage, especially if attractively decorated. Sometimes Guide and Scout Companies have their own tents and are willing to hire them out for a small fee.

Catering equipment
There is no difficulty in hiring china and cutlery from professional caterers whose names and addresses can also be found in classified telephone directories. Before spending money on this esssential item, contact local established societies such as the Women's Institute, Youth Clubs, and any other bodies who have their own premises. They may be willing to lend their crockery for a figure which is bound to be less than hiring from a professional caterer. Cardboard cups, plates and cutlery can also be bought in bulk at low prices from

Barnum's Ltd.,
67 Hammersmith Road, London, W.14.

Public address system
Contact a local radio shop if you haven't a husband, son or friend able to fix it up for you. It is a great advantage to be able to give messages, announce events and play records to get the public in the right mood. Records of British fair organs playing special fairground music are especially suitable and can be obtained from

Eroica Recording Service,
31 Peel Street,
Eccles, Manchester.

First aid
The Red Cross Society or the St. John's Ambulance Brigade will usually be pleased to man a first aid tent free of charge.

Weather insurance
Policies vary considerably and also the premiums according to the part of the country in which the event is to take place and the

time of the year when it is to be held. Insure through a local agent, or send for information about the special Pluvius Weather Insurance from

The Eagle Star Insurance Company,
1 Threadneedle Street, London, E.C.2.

Chapter 2

Fêtes and bazaars with a difference

Bon marché

Not long ago, my children arrived home from school and announced, 'We're not having a boring old fête at school this summer. It's going to be a Bon Marché, instead!'

I will never forget the glorious June day when that event was held to raise money to build the school swimming-pool. As I walked through the gates under the hoardings covered with genuine French publicity posters, the strains of the French National Anthem, the 'Marseillaise', roared in my ears. Shortly afterwards, a visiting French mistress from the Lycée Française cut the tricolour tape and declared Bon Marché open to all.

In the main courtyard were a number of boutiques and a boulangerie with long French bread, croissants and brioches; a modiste with a display of hats, scarves and gloves; pâtisseries and a wine shop with French wines. Under the trees was a *terrasse* selling soft drinks and ice-creams served by garçons, and in a corner of the Square stood Matron, dressed as a French flower-seller, selling fruit and flowers.

I know it's not easy to put on a show like this. The staff and pupils had worked for many months on this project to make it the thundering success it was. Children on holiday in France during the Easter holidays had collected newspapers, posters and advertisements. The art class had painted large and gaily illustrated notices bearing such announcements as: 'Paris Metro', 'Maison Rouge Night Club', 'Randonnées Sur La Seine', as well as election slogans on the back of the *pissoir*. Red, white and blue streamers and French flags completed the atmosphere.

How was the money raised? Sideshows included a 'treasure map' of Paris, a dartboard in the shape of a map of France and wine bottle quoits run by the children on the lawn. The model electric car-racing club, with their specially prepared Grand Prix

Fêtes and bazaars with a difference 19

race track, attracted scores of would-be racing drivers to try their hand round the circuit. There was a procession of cyclists, led by the French flag and escorted by a French policeman, followed by the Tour des Champs Cycle Race. After tea, there was a mannequin parade of dresses made in the needlework department, introduced in a broken accent by one of the senior boys. To round off the festivities, we were entertained in the evening to a first-rate French cabaret, performed in French by staff and pupils combined.

This was a tremendous achievement and would not be possible on quite such a grand scale on your village green. But the point I hope to have made is that the qualities of enthusiasm and hard work paid off. So be bold, original and energetic in your plans and once you and your committee have agreed upon an idea, let nothing put you off. Determine to carry it through and you'll soon discover that if you are confident and cheerful, it will rub off on others. No new event has ever taken place without some set-back, but solutions do turn up in the most remarkable way to those able to remain calm and single-minded in purpose.

Planning the theme and how to present it is something which can be organised months ahead. If you cast your mind back to past events you've attended, what is it that makes you remember some and forget others? Usually it is because there was a particular feature, some innovation or focal point which lifted the function out of the ordinary and so fixed itself in your memory. It is that special extra effort which endows a function with vitality and crowns it with success.

How can one set about achieving something different? First of all, by giving your fête or bazaar a title which will arouse curiosity and interest. You could adopt a theme depicting a foreign country and enlarge the scope of the function by providing the following additions:

Posters
Representative merchandise
Special foods
Music
Films
Costumes

Fêtes and bazaars with a difference

New and stimulating ideas can be collected by writing to tourist offices asking for travel brochures, posters and colourful literature giving information on their arts, crafts and traditions to help build up an authentic atmosphere. Often it is possible to borrow films free of charge also. (Addresses of Tourist Offices can be found in the London Classified Telephone Directory at all main post offices.) Many foreign countries have Food and Information Centres in our large towns and will provide special recipes and details of their countries' products which are available for sale here.

Visit your library and ask for books on the country or theme you have chosen. Cookery books, customs and folk-lore tales and others giving the geographical, historical and agricultural background. All these will help to inject new and exciting ideas into your project. Addresses of helpful societies and institutions can also be obtained from this source.

Contact local theatre and stage managers, heads of display departments from local stores and art masters teaching in schools in your area, to help you with ideas and lend you items to build up and promote your theme. It is sometimes possible to borrow an attractive advertisement, pedestals for flower arrangements, or a special window display from shops and stores. Keep your eyes open and ask for the loan of any article which will enhance the occasion you are planning.

Have you a friend with a sturdy climbing frame or some other enticing toy which you could erect in the hall, or put up in the grounds, where the fête is to take place? Ask organisations who do good work in your district if they would lend you useful attractions. The Round Tablers in our town offer their collection of swings, round-abouts, seesaws, etc., to help amuse children at charity functions. Have a corner where mothers can leave their offspring in the charge of a competent person for half an hour. This will enable them to see the stalls and select their purchases in peace.

Spend sparingly on decoration and effects and ensure that what you buy is at the lowest possible price. Crêpe paper can be obtained for as little as 8s. 6d. a dozen packets (less for larger quantities). Toys for bran tubs and gift stalls can be bought in bulk, and anything you need to hire from a megaphone, barrel organ or pennyfarthing bicycle, down to sacks for the sack race, can be obtained from Barnum's (address page 101).

Colour, too, plays a vital part and will make more impact than any other single factor. If you have adopted a particular country as a theme for your bazaar, take the colours of its flag to lend the affair meaning and to hammer the point home to your customers. Stalls can be covered in the appropriate coloured crêpe paper and the banners erected overhead in the second colour of the flag. Cardboard cut-outs denoting an emblem or specific souvenir of the country can be pinned up on the walls and painted to match. Use up any old tins of paint you may have. If you have to purchase, emulsion paint from the chain stores is the most economical and quick to dry.

Helpers (if willing) can dress in the clothes of the country and this will help enormously to unify the theme. These can be hired from Barnum's (address page 101) or made at home by adapting from ordinary dress patterns, using pictures from books as a guide.

St. Patrick's bazaar

As an illustration of a function with a special theme, here is a description of a St. Patrick's Day Bazaar. This should be held on or near the Irish National Day, March 17th, but you could hold a similar affair at any time calling it A Lucky Shamrock Sale.

Take the colours of the Irish flag which are orange, green and white. These can be made by cutting old sheets or muslin into strips and dyeing orange and green. Remember to leave some strips white. Join the three sections together on a sewing machine and nail on to a pole. Cover the stalls and tables with emerald green paper and erect orange banners over the tops of the stalls (see page 73), stating in large, white letters what goods are offered for sale. Pin up cut-outs of cardboard shamrocks, leprechauns and shillelaghs (use the sides of grocery boxes) all painted in green and orange.

For brochures, illustrated literatre, posters, other information on Ireland, and a list of films loaned free write to:

The Irish Tourist Board,
16 Mount Street, Manchester, 2.

Contact local dancing schools or a Folk Dance Society asking if they would give a performance of the Irish jig as part of an entertainment, or invite a group of singers to come along and sing some of the famous old Irish songs. If these ideas are not practical, play the music from the record 'Irish Reels' (EMI SEG 7823). A guide to recordings of folk and traditional dances from Great Britain and other countries can be obtained from

EMI Records,
EMI House,
20 Manchester Square,
London, W.1.

For books on Ireland, see what your library has to offer but here are a few titles and subjects:

My Irish Cookbook by Monica Sheridan, published by Muller.
Handbook of Old Irish Dress by McClintock, published by Dundalgan.
Irish Folk Tales by Curtin, published by Talbot Press.
History of Ireland by Chauvire, published by Clonmore.
Your Guide to Ireland by Rose, published by Redman.

Potatoes are one of the staple foods of Ireland, so make a feature offering this vegetable for sale, cooked in a variety of ways. Excellent recipes and novel ideas for cooking potatoes can be obtained free from:

The Potato Marketing Board,
50 Hans Crescent,
London, S.W.1.

Cooks can sell all their produce from the 'St. Patrick's Pantry' including Irish whisky cake, soda bread, shamrock biscuits and barmbrack currant bread.

As linen is the main product of Ireland, arrange to stock a stall specialising in the sale of linen table mats, napkins, tablecloths and teacloths, handkerchiefs and guest towels. Those with a talent for sewing will be delighted to know that a parcel containing remnants of Irish linen costing £1 can be obtained from

Copelands Linen Ltd.,
Dept. 15, Box 95,
19a Grosvenor Road,
Belfast, 12.

Regarding other ideas for things to sell, make and sew, see Chapter 7. Suggestions for entertainments, competitions and other attractions are contained in Chapter 8. But briefly, study the directory of your town, the classified telephone directory, the local papers and look up the list of associations in your area at the library. All these sources of information will enlighten you as to what goes on in your neighbourhood and who and what bodies might be able to give you practical assistance, as well as inspiration and enthusiasm to add spirit and ensure the success of your project.

Here are some more suggestions to give you ideas for variations on themes. Adapt and interpret them freely in the way most suited to your town, your public and your way of life. The titles I have given these functions do not mean that everything sold or presented at your fête is exactly representative of the theme in question. Much of the merchandise offered for sale will be the same as it has always been. The toy stall, garden produce, cakes, jumble and so on. But the point is, you will have caught the attention and imagination of the public as well as arousing their curiosity. Once you have enticed them inside, you're well on the way to persuading them to buy anything and everything.

A Caledonian market

Sell

Old jewellery, objets d'art, white elephant furniture, old clothes and jumble of all kinds. Attractive bottles suitable for lamp bases, crockery, bric-a-brac, china and glass, picture frames and records. Lavender bags, herbs, potpourri and home-made toilet water.

Decor and other attractions

Copy a gay street market with barrows and barrow-boys. Inspire the atmosphere of old London with posters of Beefeaters, the Houses of Parliament, the Tower of London or St. Paul's. Posters can be bought from The London Transport Poster Shop (address page 103). Dress somebody up as the Pearly King or Queen. Play the music of 'Big Ben Strikes Again' (EMI TWO 128). Provide plenty of strong tea, Chelsea buns and muffins sold by a Victorian street-seller clanging a bell.

Entertainment and competitions
A performance of melodrama or old time music hall songs sung by members of the committee. (See Old Time Music Hall, Chapter 3.) Hire an old movie from Wallace Heaton Ltd. (address page 102) or find an accordionist or honky-tonk player.

Run a competition for counting the nearest number of buttons on the Pearly Queen, the Knobbliest Knees or the Most Shapely Ankles.

All the fun of the fair

Sell
Toffee apples, candy, goldfish in bowls, comical noses, rick rattles, paper wavers, blow-outs, cardboard trumpets and warblers, all obtainable cheaply in bulk from Barnum's (address page 101).

Decor and other attractions
Pin up large painted cut-outs of clown faces, elephants and lions. Borrow caravans or tents and decorate them up with show-biz proclamations. 'Come inside and see the Bearded Lady.' (A man with a beard dressed up as a woman.) 'The Marvel of the Century – the Man Who's Grown Up-side-Down.' (Hire the special costume from Barnum's or make it yourself.) 'Madame Sandra Foretells Your Future.' (Book on palmistry *Palmistry—An Easy Guide to Reading Your Hand*, published by Newnes price 3s. 6d.)

Run Hoopla, roll-a-penny, coconut shies, bowling and skittles. Borrow a trampoline (enquire at Air Force Stations and Physical Education Training Centres). The Chamber of Horrors described in Chapter 6 would go down well at this function.

Entertainments and competitions
Provide a small zoo containing all the unusual animals owned by residents in your town. Give a Punch and Judy Show. Offer balloons with poster painted on-the-spot individual names.

Run a competition for the strongest man, a balloon bursting contest or a race on stilts.

Suitable demonstrations would be weight lifting, judo or an

exhibition of horsemanship by top pony riders from your local pony club.

Ye Olde Englishe fayre

Sell
English cooking from stalls with a regional flavour. Bakewell tarts, Cornish pasties, pork pies, Eccles cakes, Banburies, steak and kidney pudding, apple charlotte, dumplings, guards pudding, Victoria sponges, Sally Lunns and home-made jam.

Other special stalls can include displays of patchwork quilting, Jacobean tapestry, traditional smocking, brass rubbings from our magnificent churches and some examples of contemporary needlework and collage.

Decor and other attractions
Rig up a maypole with gay streamers twisting out to the sideshows and stalls, which can be decorated with pictures, posters or paintings of the glorious scenery of England. Hang up and dress the children in the Union Jack. Go patriotic and pin pictures everywhere of the Queens of England and play 'Rule Britannia' (Columbia SCD 2251) on the record player.

Bear in mind the hundreds of old customs and regular traditional events which take place all over the country. Gear your fête to coincide with anything held regularly nearby, providing you do not clash with the actual ceremony. For instance, Derbyshire Well-dressing Ceremonies are held in April and May; rushbearing ceremonies take place during August in Grasmere, Macclesfield and Ambleside, and there are scores of other festivals and events all over the country. To see if you have any local traditions to dig up and put to good use, look in *The B.P. Book of Festivals and Events in Britain* by Christopher Trent, published by Phoenix, available in most reference libraries.

Entertainments and competitions
Most appropriate would be a display of Morris dancing, or any of the traditional folk dances of our country, from the Hilt and Sword Dance in the North, to the Helston Floral Dance in the South. Run competitions for the best posy of wild flowers or a prize-winning photograph of beautiful Britain.

Fêtes and bazaars with a difference

Stars and Stripes

Sell:
Frilled gingham aprons, scatter cushions, novelty egg cosies and traycloths from an American Shower Gift Stall.

Cookies, gingerbread and molasses pie, barbecued hams and Chicken Maryland packed in foil containers.

Jokes and tricks, toys, Red Indian and cow-boy outfits, bows and arrows for the children.

Decor and other attractions
Rig up wigwams, totem poles and hang up the Stars and Stripes everywhere. If it's an outside event, borrow a pony and trap, build a covered wagon over the top and give rides across the prairie or through the Grand Canyon! Run a rifle range and serve hot dogs and 'coke' from a bar parlour, or waffles with maple syrup from a 'Down Town' bar.

Entertainments and competitions
Folk singers, square dancers or film shows of Walt Disney or the Wild West. Hire films from Wallace Heaton (address page 102). Organise a cow-boy and Red Indian fancy dress parade for the children. Arrange 'Lassooing the Steer', which is a traditional American contest. Provide a roped-off square and hire a donkey costume for two people. Invite spectators to try their hand at lassooing his head. If he's caught before two minutes are up the money must be returned.

A Continental bazaar

Sell:
Brightly coloured vegetables and fruit, paella in foil dishes, basketware and wrought iron flower pot holders from a stall captioned 'Spain'. Flowers and plants can be grouped together in a wheelbarrow with a helper wearing a Dutch hat and clogs.

Knitted mittens, berets, scarves and hot water bottle covers from an intriguing display of 'Goods from Scandinavia'. Include Danish pastries and dairy produce, enchanting Swedish candles or apple cake and Norwegian fish balls.

Swiss crème pâtisseries, Austrian hazel nut gâteaux, German cheese cake and Italian Biscottini from 'The Pâtisserie'.

Jumble can be cheered up by calling it 'The Paris Flea Market'.

Decor and other attractions
Paint a big black bull to depict Spain, beg a poster of the tulip bulb fields for Holland, and hoist flags of the many nations to flutter in the breeze. Serve refreshments from a gay 'Bistro' or street café and persuade your helpers to wear black berets and striped tee shirts.

Entertainments and competitions
Play the record 'Marsellaise' (Columbia SCO 2251) to welcome the public and see if one of the local dancing schools can put on a performance of the 'Can-Can'. Show Continental films borrowed from the London Tourist Offices. Invite foreign students from the local International Club to help you to serve customers and talk about their countries. Enquire if any members would be willing to dress in their national costume and sing, dance or play in the style and tongue of their country.

Run a competition for the best dressed doll depicting a Continental country. Allow the public to join in and guess the nationality of each costume.

Chapter 3

Indoor functions

Socials, dances, whist drives and theatrical productions spring instantly to mind as obvious ways in which to raise money during the winter months. So make the most of the cold weather by running a series of warm-hearted and spirited events to pass the dark evenings.

Give the functions an extra special title such as a 'Roaring Twenties Dance', a 'Hot Pot Supper', 'Beer and Skittles Evening' – these will entice the public and suggest something as good, if not better, than staying at home and watching television. Put a note at the bottom of the invitations saying, 'Transport both ways can be arranged for those without cars'. It's worth the committee organising lifts to make sure that the effort of having to walk, bus or cycle through a blizzard doesn't put anyone off at the last moment.

For all wintry events, warm the hall or rooms beforehand and try to provide something hot to eat or drink during the evening. Have plenty of bright lights, both inside and out if possible, to dispel the gloom of dreary village halls. Just a few extra bulbs make an astonishing difference and handy husbands or sons can usually be relied upon to supplement the supply, after having sought permission from the caretaker. If nothing can be done in this direction, go to the other extreme and get your effect with candles in bottles. This has the double advantage of providing a cosy and intimate atmosphere as well as making everybody look younger and more glamorous.

The amount of money you charge for entrance to socials and dances depends very much on the cost of hiring suitable premises and the payment to a band and caterers. The amount charged must cover expenses and make a profit, but will depend upon how much you can reasonably expect your public to pay. As a rough guide, here are a few figures charged for admission to various functions held in our area this year:

A St. David's Day Dance in aid of the League of Hospital Friends, held in style at the Town Hall, and including light refreshments provided by professional caterers.

    Tickets: 25s.   Profit: £120.

Victorian Music Hall Entertainment in aid of the Church Tower Fund, held in the village hall and including light refreshments prepared by the committee.

    Tickets: 7s. 6d.   Profit: £40.

Cheese and Wine Party in aid of the Spastics, held in a large country house belonging to a supporter of the Cause. Two glasses of wine allowed per person.

    Tickets: 7s. 6d..   Profit: £72.

At all these events, raffles were provided, as well as a tombola stall at the dance (see page 89), and a sales table at the Cheese and Wine Party (see page 36).

Here below are a number of celebrations which are appropriate to the winter season.

Hallow-e'en, October 31st

Hold a party for children or teenagers, inviting them to turn up in costumes with grotesque masks, broomsticks and hollowed pumpkin lanterns. Decorate a room, hall or garage on the eerie night, with branches of greenery, berries and old man's beard collected from country lanes. From the roof, hang fearful spiders, bats, snakes, cats, witches' hats and half-moons cut out of cardboard and painted black. The gruesome effect can be carried still further by lighting the proceedings with nightlights inside jam-jars, covered on the outside with green crêpe paper and by playing the record 'Haunted House Mystery Sounds and Music' (Castle HMX 1).

Sophisticated fund raisers can turn the event into a Punch Party and prepare a witches' brew to eat containing meat, red peppers and spiced herbs with curried beans and baked potatoes followed by blackcurrant tart – all spread out on a bright orange crêpe paper tablecloth.

Obvious games to play are murder, ducking for apples bobbing in pails of water and telling ghost stories. Supplement the festivities with a beat group for dancing.

St. Andrew's Day, November 30th, or
New Year's Eve, December 31st

You don't need to live North of the Border to raise funds on either of these two dates. Serve a hearty supper of Scotch broth, Haggis, Musselburgh pie or a buffet meal of Scotch eggs, oatmeal cakes and shortbread eaten to the roar of the bagpipes. If you can't find a piper, play the recorded Regimental music of 'Marching with the Royal Scots' (EMI ZLP 2072).

Have you a group of Highland Dancers in your neighbourhood? Enquire at your library and invite them to give an expert performance of the Highland Fling. Afterwards join in and dance an Eightsome Reel or the Dashing White Sergeant and celebrate the event in true Scottish style. If it's New Year's Eve, don't forget 'Auld Lang Syne' and release a shower of balloons and streamers as the clock strikes twelve.

Valentine dance, February 14th

Make this a corny, romantic, old-fashioned affair. Play sentimental music, combined with such dances as Sir Roger de Coverley, the Veleta, St. Bernard's Waltz and the Barn Dance. Include musical arms (like musical chairs with a dance in between), musical statues, elimination dances, the snowball dance, palais glide, and conga – all these and more are fun on an occasion like this.

Pin up large red, gold and white cut-outs of Valentine cards, using red crêpe paper, white doilies and gold foil. Hearts, cupids and arrows will add to the atmosphere. A sweetheart gâteau and love potion to drink will complete the celebration of this pagan festival.

Old tyme music hall

This may be a step backwards in time, but it's one of the easiest and jolliest ways of collecting money for charity. Most districts boast a group of singers who have a special repertoire of old time songs and sketches, which they are usually happy to perform for a small fee, if they are in sympathy with the cause.

Failing this, there is nothing to stop enthusiastic members from getting up their own show, but remember that you will have to pay a copyright fee if you use published material. For copies of old time songs, ballads and sketches, write to Keith Prowse Music Publishing Company (address page 104).

Books to help:

Textbook on Stagecraft by Susan Richmond, published by H. Deane, price 5s.

Guide to Greasepaint published by Samuel French, price 2s. 6d. (address page 102).

Costumes for School Plays by Barbara Snook, published by Batsford, price 16s.

It is a wise move to get the words of the songs you intend singing roneo-ed on to programme sheets. These can be sold at the door and used by guests to enable them to join in the choruses. Ask local business men, commercial firms or schools if they would be willing to give you assistance by running copies off cheaply for you.

Persuade everyone if you can to wear something Victorian or Edwardian, even if it's only a bonnet and shawl, walrus moustache and sideboards, or a velvet neckband with cameo. Best of all, of course, are Victorian bathing costumes, which can be copied from a picture or hired from Barnum's (address page 101).

Inside the hall, build up the theme with posters written on large sheets of shelf-paper, announcing 'Come to the Old Bedford'. 'Don't Dilly Dally on the Way!' 'Ta-ra-ra Boom de-ay!' Examples of illustrated music hall decor can be found in the superb book *The British Music Hall* by Mander, published by Studio Vista, which you can obtain through your public library.

Try to borrow potted palms or aspidistras, and display large jardinières or Victorian wash-stand jugs with arrangements of bulrushes and ferns. Cover small tables in bright check cloths.

The best food on these occasions is a slice of pork pie with a pickled onion, rolls and cheese, followed by a banana, apple or orange, served in a paper bag. If a licence is granted provide beer or cider, with coffee as an alternative.

New style coffee mornings

Fantastic amounts of money are raised even at ordinary coffee mornings which can be held anywhere from a small sitting-room to the Town Hall. The usual charge is 1s. for admission which includes coffee and biscuits, but most of the money made stems from the raffle and the 'Bring and Buy' sale. For the benefit of those who don't know, this is a sale run by members of the committee. The public are asked to bring an article to sell, which can be home-grown produce, items of cookery, unwanted gifts, groceries, in fact absolutely anything which might raise a few coppers. At the same time, one usually buys back an article brought by somebody else although it's not compulsory, of course. But it is surprising how often the jar of smelling salts you were given last Christmas and would never dream of using happens to be the very brand that cures Miss Barnwell's asthma. I would say that 'Bring and Buy' sales probably produce more goodwill and hard cash than any other form of amateur fund raising in the country.

To give the image of coffee mornings a bright new look, get together with your committee beforehand and plan to make yours different. Why not invite a speaker to say a few words about the cause for which you are holding the event? A short demonstration of flower arrangements in the summer, a cake icing decorating session in the early Christmas season or a talk on Spring fashions by a local stores buyer will all combine to give extra enticement to those who might otherwise not bother to come.

Very compulsive indeed are Continental Coffee Mornings. Take a country and plan your theme around it. If you choose Denmark, provide smørrebrød, Danish pastries, almond tarts, saffron bread and walnut meringues. Increase the entrance fee to 1s. 6d. to include one pastry. Any surplus left over can be sold for so much a slice, either to eat on the spot or take home.

Apply this formula to a Swiss Coffee Morning, and substitute cheese cakes, Basle cookies or chocolate gâteaux for the Danish cakes. No need to confine yourselves to the Continent either. Scottish shortbread, Dundee cakes and parkin, served at a Highland Coffee Morning, will bring everyone clamouring to buy whatever's left over. Scan the shelves containing cookery books at your library giving mouth-watering recipes for the cakes and pastries of individual regions of Britain, as well as the countries of the world.

A night in gay Paree

This event is suitable for those readers who look for an element of sophistication in their fund raising activities. One automatically thinks of such things as nightclubs and a cabaret, with perhaps a romantic encounter in the heady atmosphere of garlic, Gauloises and candlelight!

Select a hall or room with an intimate setting and scour your town or district for a group of enthusiastic amateur actresses, dancers and singers willing to get up a cabaret of songs, music and sketches in a 'Folies Bergères' style. Hire a good band by asking at your Town Hall for a list of music makers and find out from others who run dances which ones are the most popular.

Collect the young and pretty members of your society to form a bevy of seductive waitresses wearing black fishnet tights with high heeled shoes, mini-skirts and frilled aprons. See that a picture of them dressed to kill appears in a prominent position in the local paper before the event is held.

Guests can be greeted at the door by a concierge, who should direct visitors to tables bearing a small cardboard replica of the Eiffel Tower and a candle stuck in an empty wine bottle.

In a separate room captioned 'Maison Rouge Casino' provide roulette, presided over by a French croupier with a small dark moustache, red-lined cloak, rake and counters. Read the regulations governing this type of entertainment in the booklet *Voluntary Organisations and the Law relating to Lotteries and Gaming* obtainable from The National Council of Social Service (address page 103). For rules of the game, see *How to Play Roulette, Chemin de Fer, Baccarat and Blackjack* by Morris Hughes, published by Foulsham (10s. 6d.). A roulette wheel, cloth, ball, chip counters and rake can be hired from Barnum's (address page 101).

Offer a Continental-style supper of French rolls, butter, cheese and coffee which can be eaten to the strains of an accordion player, dressed in a black beret, striped tee shirt and bell bottom trousers.

A bridge drive

This can be held in a private house or small hall, either in the afternoon with the traditional cucumber sandwiches and dainty cakes and tea, or in the evening when a light buffet supper would be more appropriate.

Apart from the catering, the only organisation required is to borrow sufficient card tables, chairs, packs of cards, pencils and bridge markers. Prizes are usually donated by the committee or a supporter of the Cause.

A Bridge Drive held recently in a fairly large house in our neighbourhood, accommodated twelve tables (forty-eight players). Tickets by invitation only ensured correct numbers and cost 5s. each including tea. Each committee member supplied a plate of sandwiches or cakes and a sumptuous sponge was offered for a raffle. Profit after the remaining cakes had been sold off was £20. Not a fortune perhaps, but bridge players tend to become addicts, I'm told, and need very little persuasion to try their hand again and again.

Sausage sizzle square dance or tramps' supper

Create a rural atmosphere and beat the cold weather by running an evening of square dancing in the village hall. If you haven't an expert who can lead the dances, hire a teacher for the evening from your nearest Folk Dance and Song Society. A record player can be used with great success if you don't want the expense of hiring a band. Records, books of instruction and sheet music can be obtained from The Folk Song and Dance Society (address page 102).

If the accent is to be on the Tramps' Supper, suggest to your guests that they turn up in tramp gear. Make raggy scarecrows to hang on the walls, and prop up on the stage, and use bunches of onions, vegetables, bales of straw and the odd cartwheel to give the place a rustic look.

Knock off at half-time to consume a hearty supper of bangers and mash, or fish and chips. Entertain with a group of 'old lags' singing their favourite songs accompanied by the mouth organ, or run an impromptu sing-song of folk music.

Astrological diversion

With the recent rise in popularity of astrology, why not make an effort to turn this to good account? Nearly all magazines from the top glossies downwards run a column on this subject, which is read avidly by an enormous readership. Of course, everybody will have a tongue in their cheek, but that doesn't mean to say the evening will not be both profitable and exceedingly enjoyable.

This type of function lends itself well to a private house with several spare rooms. These will be occupied by committee members who have volunteered to read up the following books in order to take on the rather ambitious task of fortune telling in its various branches. Hide this fact from the public, and if they put their minds to it, they can remain anonymous to the end. Disguise appearances with suitable attire and hold the interviews in a faint glimmer of light. Study these books for information:

Palmistry—An Easy Guide to Reading Your Hand, published by Newnes, price 3s. 6d.

Card Fortune Telling by C. Thorpe, published by W. Foulsham, price 3s. 6d.

Astrology by Ronald Davidson, published by Arco, price 5s.

If you really want to impress people, hire a crystal ball from Barnum's, who supply character reading cards as well (address page 101).

Price of admission to this event could be fairly nominal and extra tickets sold for each separate consultation. Offer a cup of tea during the evening and throw in a reading of tea-leaves for good measure: *Teacup Fortune Telling* by Minetta, published by W. Foulsham, costs 3s. 6d.

Run a treasure hunt called 'The Missile Search', consisting of a map of the sky at night. A zodiac charm can be offered as a prize to the person who sticks a pin into the 'lucky star'.

Complete the evening by arranging for somebody with knowledge of astronomy (perhaps a schoolmaster) to give a talk on the science of the stars, with a brief history of how astronomy came to be linked with prediction and fortune telling.

A beauty demonstration

Women of all ages want to know how to make the best of themselves. Why not arrange for a Beauty Specialist to give a demonstration on skin care and the art of make-up, either in your home or in a large hall?

Large Beauty Preparation Firms if approached many months ahead may be able to send one of their consultants to clubs and societies for this purpose, or look in the local classified telephone directory and see if there are any Beauty Specialists living in your area whom you could contact. Beauty Counselors of London (address page 101) cover the country and are willing to give demonstrations in private houses to small groups of women. Expenses are charged for large groups.

Money can be raised by charging an entrance fee to include light refreshment.

A cheese and wine party

Enormously popular and easy to organise, this form of fund raising is bound to show a good profit if the homework is done properly.

If possible, persuade the owners of a gracious, stately home to allow you to hold the event in one of their elegant rooms. The whole of Britain is richly endowed with magnificent country houses which act as a tremendous draw to the public. If your Cause is a worthy one, and you have reason to believe the owner is sympathetic towards it, write and ask him if he would consider lending a room for the occasion.

The Grand House is not essential, however. Cheese and Wine parties go down well anywhere and, if combined with a tombola (see page 89), raffle (see page 14), and perhaps a sales table (see page 72), a considerable amount of money can be extracted from those who attend.

Make a special effort to set out the table attractively with a variety of cheeses, bread and celery. Well-known chain stores will prepare a selection of cheeses at competitive prices. Ideas for presenting the snacks can be obtained from the booklet *Cheese and Wine Parties*. Write for a free copy to The English Country Cheese Council. (address page 102). Arrange for somebody to decorate the place with attractive pedestals and bowls of flowers which can be auctioned at the end of the party to help swell the profits.

The simplest way to run this type of party is to send out invitations stating that the occasion is in aid of a particular charity. Ask your wine merchant to supply the bottles on a sale or return basis. Glasses are usually loaned free of charge for the event from the same source.

Chapter 4

Outdoor functions

Summer is the time when money-making entertainment comes into its own. Sunshine and the lush green countryside promote an atmosphere of generosity and the happy-go-lucky feeling that goes hand-in-hand with successful enterprises.

Bear in mind the activities which can be enhanced by bounteous nature when you plan outdoor functions. Are there any beautiful gardens in your district, whose owners might be prepared to lend them as a setting for a charitable occasion? If you live near an attractive river, why not hold a Water Carnival, and if you are lucky enough to be near the sea run a Beach Bonfire Party with a barbecue, sing-song and fireworks?

In some parts of the country where there is a strong pony club element, it would pay to put on a gymkhana. But don't undertake to run one without the full support of an experienced horsewoman who will handle the special organisation necessary for an event of this kind. The same applies to a tennis or golf championship which can also be held to augment funds.

The fact must be faced, however, that our climate can devastate a carefully planned event and turn it into a disaster, so prepare to shift the proceedings under cover if shelter is available. It is possible to sell £20 worth of cakes from a leaking garden shed during a three hour deluge of rain! I've done it, but often there are better alternatives and it is wise to investigate every possibility. Some organisers advertise the fact that if it rains, the event will be held the following week or day. Most of us though, grit our teeth and determine to carry on, come what may. Weather insurance policies have been dealt with on page 16.

Here are some further suggestions for summer fund raising.

A strawberries and cream tea
I know somebody whose strawberry beds yield large quantities of these delectable fruits. She shares her good fortune annually

by holding a Strawberry Tea, the profits going to the local 'Over Sixties' club.

This event must be held when the strawberries are most likely to be at their best. In the Home Counties, this time will fall during the last two weeks in June, but naturally this differs in various parts of the country. Find out when the height of your season takes place by asking the advice of local fruit growers.

A certain amount of subterfuge is required in order to make these choice, expensive fruits go a long way. No profit will be shown if a large bowl of strawberries and cream are offered to each customer in return for a 3s. 6d. ticket. Make every strawberry earn its weight in hard cash, by using them as decorations in a number of different ways. Home-baked scones can be offered ready spread with strawberry jam and a dab of cream. Sponges and small cakes can be embellished on top with the best strawberries, set amid exotic whirls of piped cream. Serve individual strawberry jellies and small open pastry tarts containing two or three of these precious fruits, covered in glaze.

A remarkably simple way of economising on the quantity of cream required and making it stretch much further without destroying the consistency or flavour can be achieved by the following method. Beat two or three egg whites until fairly stiff. Add a tablespoon of sugar and beat again. Whip one pint of cream until fluffy, but not buttery, and lightly fold in the egg whites.

Provide a raffle which could be for a strawberry gâteau or flan and sell surplus jam, jellies and scones, as well as running a 'Bring and Buy' sale (see page 32) to help the afternoon's profits along.

A Madeira morning

This function is a sophisticated version of the coffee morning and requires less effort to prepare and serve. Invite guests to drink Madeira wine and ask them for a donation. Visit your wine merchant and see what he has to offer for this particular occasion.

I think this event calls for a Portugese or Spanish atmosphere which can easily be achieved by holding the party outside and hanging up trophies and souvenirs brought back from holidays. Whether you wear a sombrero and play 'Spanish Fire' (Mercury

MMC 14121) on your record player is up to you. But sell brightly coloured fruit, flowers and vegetables and offer home-cooked paella and Andalusian salad in foil containers for customers to take home and eat for lunch. Provide a large Madeira cake to raffle (see page 14).

For the less ambitious, money can be raised equally well at ordinary sherry mornings run in the same fashion. If you prefer, hold a similar function in the evening and call it a Sundowner Party.

Sponsored walks

The organisation of a sponsored walk should begin with a write-up in the local newspaper, featuring the name of a well-known personality in the district who is willing to give his or her name to add authority to the project. The fact that this person is giving support to the march will make all the difference to the number of sponsors likely to come forward. Give full details of the proposed route, where and when it is to take place and ask for volunteers to come forward. Display posters all over the district giving the same information.

Once the event is well established in the minds of your public, it is up to each person intending to embark on the walk to get as many sponsors for himself as possible. A sponsor usually offers to pay between 3d. and 2s 6d. for every mile covered. Local firms can be approached for support as well as notable personalities and all those interested in the Cause.

Arrangements must be made with the police to control traffic if necessary. Negotiate with the St. John's Ambulance Brigade to provide first aid and marshals must be found to check the walkers at certain points on the journey. Willing helpers are needed with cars to pick up those who fall by the wayside and also for transporting marchers back to base afterwards. To get over this problem, it is good fun to organise a circular walk such as 'Beating the Bounds' of your town or Parish. A search through the records at your library should provide much interest historically and offer a more personal appeal to the affair.

Contact all the villages or towns through which the march passes, so that money can be collected en route. Long poles with nets, collecting tins and sacks can be carried, so that those in

40 Outdoor functions

cars and by the way can throw in coins. It is usual for some of the volunteers to carry banners stating the cause they're supporting. Weird garments and headgear worn by the leaders help to attract attention, too.

Each walker should be issued with a form before the walk takes place, to ensure that his sponsors sign a pledge to pay up after the feat has been achieved (see figure 1). Sometimes, I regret

Name	Address	Amount Sponsored Per Mile	Signature	Paid

Fig. 1. A sponsorship form for an organised walk

to say, sponsors have been known to try to escape handing over the full amount. A glance at their own signature against the figures usually solves the problem.

A safari party

I consider this to be a brilliant way of avoiding the hard work of entertaining and cooking at home for a large number of people. A Safari Party, or Progressive Party as it is sometimes called, enables everyone, including the host and hostess, to enjoy themselves to the full and raise some money at the same time.

The evening's entertainment begins in the first house with sherry, canapés and perhaps the first course of soup or *hors d'oeuvre*. The company then proceeds to the next home for the main dish and another for the dessert. Whether or not it moves on yet again for cheese and biscuits and coffee, depends on the organisers. It is a great help if they live fairly close to one another, in which case the entire proceedings can take place on foot. Otherwise transport must be provided.

It is usual to charge an overall figure for this progressive feast, and it should take into account the cost of the food, drink and petrol if cars are used.

A market stall

Is there an open market in your town? If so, have you thought of applying to the market superintendent at your council offices for permission to run a stall there one morning for the benefit of your Charity?

Sometimes stalls are booked up months in advance, so plan well ahead. The cost is minimal (10s. for the day in our square), and you can hardly fail to make a profit under these circumstances, even if it rains the whole time.

Home-baked cooking is probably the most popular and saleable commodity. Sufficient effort must be made to persuade your cooks to provide enough goodies to sell, because the cry is usually, 'If only we'd cooked more'. There is seldom anything left over as demand always exceeds supply.

Antiques, white elephants, bric-a-brac and all second-hand articles will sell rapidly on a market stall too. We collected £68 in one morning by this method for our Mentally Handicapped Association. The reason for this sell-out was put down to the fact that the public expects to buy this kind of merchandise when visiting a street market and is therefore 'tuned in' to the idea of spending money in this way.

While on the subject of markets, remember that the regular stall holders provide an excellent source of supply for all charity functions. Not only do they offer goods at rock bottom prices, but as a rule they're sympathetic, interested and anxious to help good causes in any way they can.

A treasure hunt

A ramble across country, with carefully laid clues leading finally to a member's house or a pub for beer and sandwiches, is a

42 Outdoor functions

delightful way to bring in money on a long, light summer's evening.

Divide the company into three or more groups according to the numbers present, giving each group a set of clues marked with their number – 1, 2 or 3. Prepare these beforehand and place strategically on the route. Give each party a sealed envelope before leaving with the name of the destination inside. This can be opened at a given time – just in case they lose their way.

The clues laid will depend on your district, but most neighbourhoods possess road signs, an unusual tree, gravestones, post and telephone boxes. Try to make the rhymes witty, amusing and slightly cryptic. For instance, a clue leading to a graveyard could run:

'Upon the hill,
Beneath the yews,
The howling wind
Cools dead men's shoes.'

To add to the fun, include one or two items to be collected en route, such as a snail, an ear of barley, a couple of thistles, a theatre programme or a large toadstool.

Arrange with the landlord in advance if you plan to finish the evening at a pub, but more profit will be shown if you revive the party privately. Either way, lay on some traditional pub games. Read *The Watney Book of Pub Games* by Timothy Finn, published by Queen Anne Press (11s. 6d.) which gives instructions on how to play shove ha'penny, darts, dominoes, marbles, table skittles and tossing the penny.

A brunch party

Hold an informal Brunch Party one summer Sunday morning and raise money by giving supporters of your cause a rest from cooking breakfast and lunch. This function can be held on a small patio or garden lawn, with deck chairs, hammocks, lots of cushions and a general air of relaxation. Use cheerful china and pottery and bowls of fresh fruit set on colourful check cloths, and cook the eggs, bacon and coffee on a picnic stove outside for guests as they arrive.

Follow this up with a Quoit Tennis Tournament to keep the

party spirit in full swing. A court can be fitted on to a patch of lawn about 9 × 5 yards (see figure 2) measured out with string and marked over with whitewash and brush if you can't borrow a marker. Two bamboo poles and a piece of string fixed at a height of 6 feet will serve as a net. A quoit is a rubber ring which can be bought for a few shillings from a sports shop. The rules are practically the same as for tennis apart from the fact that the arm should not be raised above the shoulder in service or return.

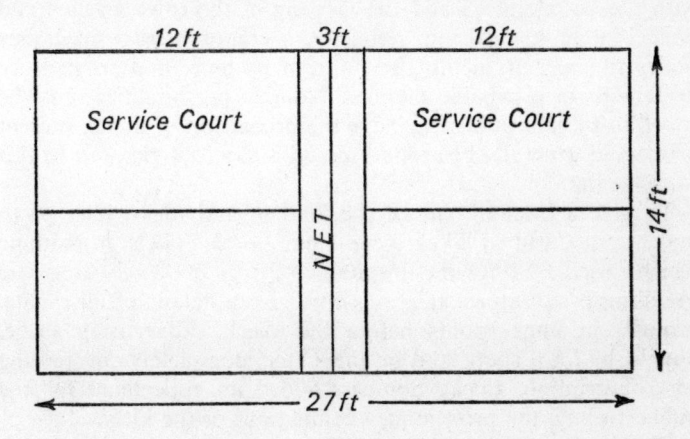

Fig. 2. A quoit tennis court

Provide soft drinks at a price, to refresh your guests between contests. Don't forget a raffle (see page 14) and a tombola (see page 89) to make extra profit. If rain should fall on this occasion, a Table Tennis Tournament is a good alternative.

A carnival

What exactly is a Carnival? It is a lavish, colourful and garish spectacle laid on by an enthusiastic number of fund raisers to entertain and catch the public's fancy in order to gather a large sum of money for a worthy cause. Some Carnivals last for a week, others concentrate all the festivities into one uproarious Saturday. If there are lots of tireless teenagers and young people in your

44 Outdoor functions

district, go all out for a week or several days of junketing and merry-making events.

The theme should be one of gaiety and fun, a galaxy of crazy and enchanting feasts for the eye, the days packed with fast-moving activity of one sort or another and the nights spent dancing in wild abandon under the stars, with fireworks, bonfires and barbecues thrown in for good measure.

A large and competent committee is essential for the mammoth task of preparation and the entire undertaking must be planned with the co-operation and the blessing of the town council and police force. Advertising, publicity, a comprehensive insurance policy to cover accidents, these and many more matters must be dealt with in a capable manner. Notable personalities must be roped in to gain publicity, judge the procession of floats, present prizes and generally be around to add a touch of glamour to this extravaganza.

To give a brief outline of the kind of activities which go to make up a Carnival Week, here is our Local Yokels programme which raised £600 for the hospital.

Selling programmes at 2s. a copy, giving details of all events, brought in huge profits before the Week. Advertising space, bought by local shops and business men, completely covered the cost of printing. Lucky numbers added an enticement for the public to buy, the prize money coming out of the kitty.

First event of the week was a Tournament on our river which happens to flow beside the market, where shoppers were out in full swing. Two home-made rafts bore a couple of jousters apiece, all bearing long-handled mops and intent upon the one idea of pushing their opponents into the water. Replacements were substituted until one team managed to gain complete victory.

This contest, apart from the few coins collected by passing tins round the audience was not a large money-raiser, but the attention it attracted gained a tremendous public and placed the idea of the Carnival firmly into the minds of all those who saw it.

A Barbecue and Beat night took place at a nearby farm during the evening, and next day a Bicycle Polo Match was fought on the green. The following evening saw a first-class presentation at the Town Hall of an intimate revue, given by a company of amateurs. On Friday, the famous annual hair-raising Pram Race, where decorated prams containing large 'babies' pushed by tough, manly competitors, racketed round a pre-planned town route at break-neck speed. A Jazz Bonanza concluded this day's activities and a Comedy Rugby Match, a Procession of Floats and a Grand Carnival Ball wound up the week of festivities in suitably riotous fashion.

Decorated floats
Whether you are organising or merely taking part in one of these glittering, spectacular processions, there is a great deal of fun and profit to be extracted from the project. Considerable pleasure will also be given to those who line the pavements to marvel at the strange and impressive sights.

Those in charge of planning the arrangements should write several months ahead to all industrial firms, clubs, associations and any other members of the public who live in the district and might be interested. Inform them of the date and enclose a preliminary entry form giving particulars of the classes of entry. When these are returned, it is up to the organisers to send back a route sheet and supply further details.

Concerning the actual decoration of the floats, the first practical consideration is to find your lorry and driver. This can usually be arranged by contacting local firms and asking if they would co-operate. The lorry will be required on the evening before the event, in order to transform it into the prize winning effort.

There will probably be several different classes of entry, but whichever you choose, the basic principles are the same. Try to make a strong impact with two or three vivid colours – an important but often overlooked fact. To achieve this, use strongly dyed muslin, old sheets or curtains. Don't be tempted to use crêpe paper as this tears to shreds in the wind and is ruined by a downpour of rain.

Study books and illustrations relating to your theme from the public library. Build the tableau to face the sides of the lorry, so that onlookers watching from the pavements can see the full effect and do not build any structure too high, lest it topples over.

Titles of the classes of entry will probably include 'artistic', 'humorous' and 'topical'. Decorate an artistic float to depict 'fashion through the ages' by presenting models wearing the clothes of a stone-age man, an ancient Briton, an Elizabethan, a Victorian and an Edwardian and bring up to date with an ultra-modern style. Scenes from books, films, shows and plays also fall into this category and offer competitors plenty of scope.

'Heaven and hell' makes a marvellous tableau for a humorous float. Red-horned devils can drink champagne and play roulette among tongues of fire on one half of the lorry, while angels grouped on the other half kneel between golden gates plucking harps or praying in long, white winged gowns. The awful girls of 'St. Trinian's' cause quite a stir too, with pupils dressed in grey gym slips, school panamas, orange ties and matching hat bands. The many captions on blackboards can proclaim 'Down with Teacher', 'We Want Co-Education' and so on.

Ideas for topical floats must spring from the newspapers. Pick a hero of our time like Sir Francis Chichester standing at the tiller of a boat resembling 'Gipsy Moth' or 'The Common Market' showing the Channel Tunnel, with the Prime Minister on one side and the Continentals on the other.

Ensure money is extracted from the public by supplying long poles with capacious nets to those on the float and provide sturdy walkers to rattle the collecting tins. If they are dressed in similar attire it will be possible for them to change places with those on the lorry when they're tired of running beside it.

A stomp and sheep roast

Find a friendly farmer to lend a field and use gentle persuasion on a sympathetic butcher and organise a profitable and unusual evening's entertainment.

A 'Stomp' is officially a jazz dance characterised by heavy stomping and originated from Oklahoma tribesmen. But any energetic square or folk-dancing will fill the bill, so ask at your library for the address of your nearest Folk Dance Society. Invite a member to help and advise you on planning the evening and to play the role of 'caller' on the night of the function.

Try to arrange for a sheep or calf to be roasted on this occasion. Nothing compares with the special delight of sitting on bales of straw munching a chunk of meat between bread rolls, and watching the roasting animal rotating on its spit above the red hot coals. If you can't procure the services of a butcher or someone else competent to undertake to roast a whole animal, lay on a barbecue instead. Serve up hot dogs, baked beans, potatoes in jackets, lamb kebabs and hot cheese and ham rolls. Full instructions for constructing and cooking on a barbecue can be found in *The Art of Barbecue and Outdoor Cookery* by The Tested Recipe Institute, published by Bantam (4s. 6d.).

Run a lucrative taxi service home on a hay cart pulled by a horse or tractor. What better way to end the festivities than a lazy wagon ride beneath the starry, moonlit sky?

Chapter 5

Seasonal fund raising

Functions held at Festival and Bank Holiday times are invariably successful money-spinners. Whenever the Nation is on holiday, large numbers of people will have time on their hands. Try to fill this void by providing money-making entertainment to profit your Cause.

Christmas is an especially rewarding period for the fund raiser. Fancy dress dances, a grand poultry whist drive, carol singing, Christmas stalls and fairs will all bring successful results. Choral, orchestral and organ concerts held in churches are very popular at this time of the year but naturally, the special collection on these occasions would be donated to the Church funds, or to a charity of which the Vicar approves.

Arrest the attention of the public at Easter, by organising an Easter bonnet parade, reviving an old custom or running a stall on the market selling home-made hot cross buns. Cash in at this time on the annual Spring fever which sweeps the country and attacks housewives everywhere. The great wave of enthusiasm for new furnishings and household articles can be turned to good account. Old clothes too will be thrown out and this will enable you to stock up your jumble stall. At the other end of the fashion market, Spring Fashion Parades cannot fail to draw a large audience.

Summer events have been covered in previous chapters (Fêtes and Bazaars with a Difference, Chapter 2, and Outdoor Functions, Chapter 4) but two further suggestions could be adapted and used as an added attraction to any fête. A May Day Miscellany offering a display of dancing round the maypole, followed by a Queen of the May Beauty Competition, and a Mid-summer Revel centred around an exhibition of Morris Dancers. For those wishing to raise money for their Church, festivals of flowers draw vast numbers of people. The magnificent displays of floral arrangements set against the background of our beautiful churches are without parallel in the pleasure they give to the public. Flower

Arrangement Societies must be approached to see if they are willing to undertake the formidable task of decoration.

Autumn is the time when thoughts are turning to winter hobbies and ways in which to fill the long, dark evenings. One looks back with nostalgia to the summer (holiday transparencies make money!) and forward to preparations for Christmas.

Here then are some ideas with special reference to the seasons.

Spring

A house and garden gala

This is the time of the year when change is in the air and new brooms sweep everywhere clean. At this turning out of homes be ready to cash in and acquire unwanted items by collecting them and selling them as white elephants. Incorporate an exhibition of flower arrangements as well to promote the theme of Spring and beauty in the home. If you haven't a Flower Arrangement Society near you to help mount a show, at least provide a few displays of daffodils and blossom to set the scene.

Suggestions for articles to make and sell can be found in Chapter 7, but concentrate on offering gaily coloured household articles. Bright matching sets of table linen, arrayed in style with candles and flowers to tone, will catch the public's eye. Tray cloths, trolley cloths, tea cosies, and aprons and cushions in all shapes and sizes made from remnants of gingham or cotton sell like wildfire. Lampshades and lamp bases, created from attractive wine and chianti bottles, bewitching collage pictures and banners, fashioned from scraps of material or felt, make a splash of colour and a novel display. Include a stall selling remnants of material, trimmings, buttons and bits and pieces which may come in handy for the needlewoman. Try to have a Bargain Box where no article costs more than 6d. or 1s. This is very popular with children and other members of the community who simply cannot afford to spend lavishly.

A bathroom stall can be stocked with such things as toilet and make-up bags made cheaply from quilted plastic; travel packs containing soap, flannel and small towel; bath cleaners made of net (see page 80); loose bath salts jazzed up in discarded jars tied with bright ribbon, and plastic tooth mugs decorated in washable paints.

Remember the kitchen on this occasion and paint empty tins of every conceivable kind to hold biscuits, other foodstuffs, tea or string, using transfers to enhance the effect. Meat tins (obtainable from friendly butchers) make marvellous waste paper bins and can be covered with odd pieces of cretonne or wallpaper and covered with a coat of clear varnish. Used baby food jars can be made into attractive sets of spice containers, by painting each one with vertical stripes and labelling individually with transfers. See if you can scrounge some pottery rejects from amateur potters in the neighbourhood. Ask your china shops, too, for their seconds or throw-out items of china.

A stall offering decorative containers of any kind suitable for flowers, will attract flower arrangers like a magnet. Ask your friends to look in their attics and scour old junk shops during the months before the Gala for Victorian soup tureens, soap dishes, candlesticks, washbasins and jugs, sea-shells, odd wine glasses, plates and dishes. Figurines too, even if cracked or damaged, will be much sought after and carried away by triumphant customers.

Garden lovers will come into their own running a stall stocked with annual seedling plants such as larkspur, asters, lobelias, pansies and clarkia. Phlox, varieties of michaelmas daisies, chrysanthemums, peonies and other perennials are often separated at this time of the year and are much in demand. Snowdrop bulbs, lilies-of-the-valley, ivy and geranium cuttings, all in pots, sell rapidly to keen gardeners.

Set up an enticing corner offering an attractive selection of herb plants such as lavender, rosemary, rue, chives, mint, parsley, thyme and sage. Dried herbs can be sold too. Sell items of food containing herbs and spices as well, like coriander honey cakes, herb scones, poppy seed cake, saffron buns and spiced biscuits. Potpourri packaged in pretty containers, pomander balls (see page 74), rose petal jam and crystallised mint leaves would all add interest to this particular theme. Advice and information on the above subjects can be found in the book *Herbs and Spices* by R. Hemphill, published by Penguin (4s. 6d.).

An Easter frolic

There are still many traditional customs which are carried out every Easter. Orange rolling attracts scores of onlookers on Dunstable Downs every year, egg-rolling ceremonies survive in the North of England, and Baccup 'Nutters' in Lancashire perform weird and strange dances on Easter Saturday. A Marbles Championship has been held at Tinsley Green in Sussex since Elizabethan times, and a Bottle Kicking and Pie Scramble in Leicestershire provides spectators with a tough, exciting battle to watch on Easter Monday. Why not put on a spectacle in your town to draw the crowds and arouse interest in a day of festivities?

The Frolic could begin with a revival of one of these events. Investigate possibilities by reading up Easter traditions and customs at your library. Incorporate an Easter Fayre or set up stalls selling the time honoured Easter food, such as hot cross buns, simnel cakes, flower bedecked sponges, Easter biscuits and eggs offered in every conceivable way. Chocolate eggs, Scotch eggs, egg and cheese flans and eggs decorated and painted for fun attract the most attention and a leaflet giving instructions can be obtained free from The British Egg Marketing Board (address page 101).

Another stall could be stocked with small flower arrangements in empty painted meat or fish tins, covered with moss and filled with primroses and other simple country flowers. Tiny baskets and strawberry punnets make ideal containers for this purpose too.

Provide a competition for the children called 'Guess the Lucky Egg'. Place a number of broken egg shell halves, up-side-down on some egg packing cartons or racks. Put 6d. or 1s. underneath some of the shells and charge 3d. a time for competitors to find 'lucky eggs'.

A hat and hair-style parade

A Millinery Parade or a Show of Hair-Styles is an obvious choice for an Easter entertainment, but much will depend on your local resources.

Contact hairdressers and milliners in the neighbourhood and discuss the possibility of arranging a combined project. It is usual to devote one half of the Show to each speciality. Further details of arrangements can be found in the description of the Champagne Fashion Show below.

A mad hatters' ball

Invite all attending this function to arrive in a home-made creation of cardboard, decorative paper, feathers and other accessories, fashioned into some kind of headwear – the more fantastic the better. Men are not excluded from this contest and can seek inspiration either from the elaborate styles of the past, or by conjuring up ideas for space helmets of the future. Offer prizes in the form of vouchers for new Spring hats, one for the most ornamental, another for the most original and a third for the best executed. The manageress of a local millinery store or department can be asked to judge the results.

Decorate the hall with cardboard cut-outs of Alice-in-Wonderland characters – white rabbits and large watches, huge teapots and sleepy dormice. Link up each motif by hanging garlands of thin strips of green and yellow paper twisted together. Bowls of daffodils, narcissi and forsythia, mixed with pussy willow and delicate sprays of blossom will add to the overall effect of an Easter and Spring theme.

A champagne fashion show

Fortunately female fashions change constantly and the public's demand for new styles in clothes is insatiable. All over the country, Fashion Shows are turning out to be gold mines for fund raisers. Tickets at 5s. or 7s. 6d. each are usually sold out before the event takes place and the organisers realise with glee that in a few months, the same audience will be clamouring for more.

Most Fashion Shows for charity are arranged in conjunction with local departmental stores, dress shops or boutiques. Investigate this possibility first and ask in your neighbourhood. Sometimes large nation-wide stores such as Marks & Spencer will co-operate with an undertaking of this nature, but these can only be arranged if there is a guaranteed audience of at least one thousand. Naturally such firms are booked up very much in advance and negotiations must take place well before the time planned.

The encouraging fact remains, that apart from the cost of hiring the hall, organising the advertising, selling the tickets, providing flowers, background music, refreshments and perhaps the cat-walk, the entire cost of the Parade is usually borne by the store or shop in question.

Therefore your problems are easily surmountable. Hire a large hall with sufficient seating accommodation and facilities for running a champagne or coffee bar. Champagne or a substitute sparkling wine can be sold for so-much-a-glass during the interval providing you can arrange with a licencee to serve it. Approach your Flower Arrangement Society for help with enhancing the hall. Check that a public address system is available or make arrangements for this to be installed. Music can be tape recorded previously and played softly in the background.

Ask an attractive V.I.P. to open the event, thereby lending a touch of glamour to the occasion. Provide a raffle (see page 14) the winner to receive a voucher for £5–£10 worth of clothes, to be bought from the store sponsoring the Show.

This only leaves the rather vexed question of how to provide a carpeted cat-walk. Although a raised structure is not essential, it does ensure that everyone has a clear view of the models as they display the clothes. Hall caretakers or handy husbands usually rise to the occasion by rigging up something suitable, such as a number of identical tables placed end to end. A long length of carpet or covering is essential, in order to protect long dresses from the floor. Try your local carpet stores who can sometimes help out, but you may have to resort to hiring both cat-walk and covering from a marquee supplier. If the affair has been put on to raise money for a church, the Minister may be willing to lend you the length of carpet which graces his aisle.

Autumn

A Michaelmas mart and hobbies fair

Do-it-Yourself Exhibitions draw large crowds in the big cities. Promoting interest and enthusiasm for arts, crafts and creative hobbies can pull in the public, especially at this time of the year when winter looms ahead. Money can be made by running the usual bazaar stalls, raffle (see page 14), tombola (see page 89), and refreshments, with the added attraction of purchasing home-produced crafts made by the experts.

Where do you find these talented people? If you don't already know any, contact the editor of your local paper who will probably astound you with the number of unusual craftsmen and women living in your district. Invite these people to demonstrate their work at the show. This is the point of a Hobbies Fair – to give the public an opportunity to see how it's done. Quilting, leather tooling, painting, smocking, cake decoration, weaving, jewellery making, rug hooking – all these and a host of other hobbies will fascinate and gather an audience. If some of the finished results are on show and for sale, so much the better. If not, orders could be taken and delivered in the future for the benefit of the cause if the craftsman is willing, but the charm of such an occasion lies in the inspiration it offers to onlookers. New ideas or the stimulation of a fresh outlet for creative energy draws together those who would otherwise be denied this pleasure.

Offer a sumptuous display of harvest fruits, flowers and vegetables to sell at this event. A table selling home-made preserves and pickles made from traditional recipes like crab apple jelly, pickled cabbage, pickled onions, mint jelly and tomato or apple chutney are usually a sell-out.

Dried flowers and leaves are much in demand for home decoration at this time when fresh flowers become expensive. Beech and laurel leaves can be preserved in a jar containing equal parts of glycerine and boiling water. Seed heads, hydrangeas, larkspur, delphiniums and achillea only need to be picked at their prime and hung upside down at room temperature until completely dry. The life of berries, of hips and haws, pyracantha and cotoneaster will be prolonged by applying colourless nail varnish. Artichokes, bulrushes, cape gooseberries, thistles and gourds will also find a ready market.

Competitions could be run to augment the theme of home-crafts. A prize given for the best-dressed doll, a picture of a local scene depicted in any medium, an article made from not more than one yard of gingham or the most attractive piece of patchwork.

Holiday memories

It is more than likely that you know several people who own superb collections of transparencies taken whilst on holiday abroad, or indeed in this country.

Film shows of this nature can be organised in a friendly, simple way and held in private homes without incurring any expense at all. Guests are happy to pay a few shillings for this entertainment, especially if a buffet supper is provided by the joint efforts of those supporting the charity.

Musical evenings can be arranged in a similar fashion. Most of us number musicians among our acquaintances and with a little effort they can usually be persuaded to give performances of their prowess. Do remember to thank those who have given their time and talents for your cause in an official speech during the course of the evening.

An evening book sale

Everybody it seems can rustle up a few books from their shelves to give away. On the other hand the prospect of the winter months ahead encourages the bookworm to stock up his bedside table with fresh reading matter. Why not invite these two groups of people to co-operate and provide a Book Sale? Add authority and interest to the occasion by inviting a local bookseller to give a short, constructive talk on the subject of books and reading.

Early collection by the organisers is essential in order to sort the books into categories and mark them clearly with the appropriate prices. Advertise the Sale to schools, colleges and institutions as well as in the columns of the local press. Classify the collection into sections similar to the following:

Children's stories.
Novels, thrillers and detective stories.
Travel, adventure and biography.
Educational.
House, garden and hobbies.
Miscellaneous.

Sell old journals, glossies and comics from 'The Magazine Stall'.

From my experience it appears that people go mainly for the paperbacks. This is presumably because they feel the price will be lower than for a hardback copy, therefore price accordingly. Keep the overall figures low, from 3d. to 2s. for the ordinary books.

Ask your speaker if he would be kind enough to cast his eye over the books beforehand in order to pick out any which might be of value. It is just possible that a rare edition might come your way. And suggest tactfully that during the course of his talk, he directs the attention of his listeners towards some of the books offered for sale. A knowledgeable expert in this field can make all the difference to the success of the evening.

Christmas

A toy fair

Discarded toys collected well before the Festive Season and offered for sale at a Toy Fair can provide a magnificent solution for thrifty parents who are on the look-out for bargain presents to give their off-spring. At the same time it brings in healthy profits to the organisers for the small outlay of hiring a hall.

The secret of success lies entirely in the effort expended on the toys beforehand. Many will need repair (husbands and sons can help), others require just spit and polish and some will benefit from a coat of paint.

Pack old jig-saws into new boxes with attractive Christmas labels. Doll lovers will delight in making fresh outfits to replace tatty clothes and soft toys will need washing. Crayons, pencils, rulers, pens and rubbers can be made up into sets and sold in plastic containers. Sell odd beads in transparent bags with needle and thread included, ready for small girls to fashion necklaces and bracelets. Oddments of all kinds can be packaged together and sold for 6d. The possibilities and scope for the imagination are endless.

A most unusual and striking raffle prize which can be made beforehand is guaranteed to fill any small child with rapture (see figure 3). It is a fabulous, gold turreted castle easily constructed on a large cake board and offered with an attached box of sweets or toffees. (State clearly the amount offered.)

Place an upturned box or tin in the centre of the board, build up and glue on a series of turrets and towers. These can be

Seasonal fund raising 57

discarded cylindrical objects such as the centres of aluminium foil packets or Squeezy bottles or made with sheets of cartridge paper stuck with cow gum to form a cylinder. Make cone turrets and roofs from a circle of paper or cardboard and stick to the tops of the cylinders. (See figure 3.) When completed, spray the whole structure with gold paint, and add silver doily edges to turrets and battlements when the paint has dried.

A stairway of folded cartridge paper can be glued to the centre of the cake base leading to a door etched in with a felt-tipped pen. Windows and other appropriate embellishments can be

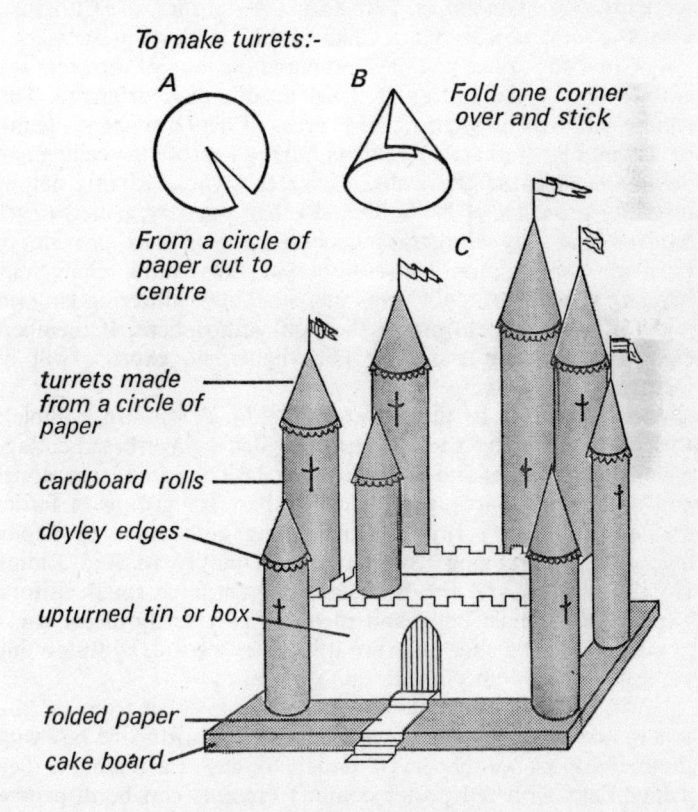

Fig. 3. A gold turreted castle

added this way. Complete with a flourish of matchstick flagstaffs surmounted by colourful paper flags.

A Christmas grotto

This is a hard method of raising cash, but the special magic of Christmas, reflected in the joy and response of the children who throng to see this fantasy, makes the project worth any amount of sweated labour.

Is there an empty shop near the centre of your town? Find out from the owner if you can borrow it for a day or a whole week preceding Christmas. Transform the interior into a Christmas Grotto complete with Santa Claus and his sack of presents.

The first step, once you have procured the loan of the premises, is to lower the ceiling to give the effect of a cave or grotto. This can be achieved by securing large areas of net (strawberry, tennis or fishing nets – whatever you can borrow) across the ceiling and down the sides of the walls. Cover the whole of this net by inserting branches of fir, holly and other greenery, cones, tinsel, baubles and any Christmas decorations you can provide or borrow. Large murals or cut-outs of fairy book characters, hanging mobiles of 'cube' presents, stockings, glittering lanterns and foil stars help to create the right atmosphere. If members club together and lend their fairy lights, no expense will be incurred for this item.

A tea chest can be turned into a Goldilock's house, complete with three bears and another into the witch's gingerbread cottage which lured Hansel and Gretel to look inside. Some large stones and moss can be arranged to form a base for groups of fairies and elves. Nursery rhyme scenes using dolls, toys or papier mâché figures ranging from Humpty Dumpty to Red Riding Hood and Jack and the Beanstalk will entrance small visitors. Tape record 'Jingle Bells' and carols to play softly in the background. Borrow a slide and turn it into a snow run, by festooning with cotton wool and foil icicles.

Santa Claus can emerge with considerable effect from the top of a mock chimney pot. Cover a tall narrow cardboard box with simulated brick wallpaper. (If somebody hasn't a remnant, then paint bricks with red poster colour.) Presents can be dispensed from a quantity of sacks marked 'Boy' or 'Girl'.

For help in dealing with this enormous part of the undertaking, write to Barnum's (address page 101). This firm has a comprehensive scheme designed to assist organisers of children's functions of all kinds. Give particulars of your project, together with the amount you wish to spend, the number of presents you require, for which sex, and the approximate age group. They will do the rest, by selecting suitable presents from their large, labelled, wholesale stocks. Send for their catalogue 'Gifts for Children' and further details of this time and money-saver.

A Yuletide bonanza bazaar

Highlight the Festive Season in your community by brow-beating the public to shop and spend for Christmas in your bazaar, thereby benefiting a worthy cause at the same time. Advertise the fact that you can provide gifts galore, seasonal food, decorations for the house, table and tree, as well as presents and a Santa Claus for the children.

Stalls should be brightly decorated with red crêpe paper and other Christmas decorations and clearly marked FESTIVE FOOD, XMAS TREE DECORATIONS, CHILDREN'S GIFT STALL, and so on. Run a bottle tombola (see page 89), provide Santa Claus with sacks of presents (see above for where to buy toys wholesale), and dispense tea and mince pies to tape recorded music of Christmas carols.

Dolls, animals, gonks and soft toys of all kinds will bring much joy to small recipients. Pipe-cleaner animals and figures, choir boys made from cardboard, robins on small pieces of tree bark with a sprig of holly and one or two baubles, will enchant the young too. Gift stalls can stock and sell every conceivable object, including your last year's unwanted presents! More ideas and suggestions for making gifts can be found in Chapter 7.

Food is firmly to the forefront of everybody's minds at this time. Apart from the usual and obvious items like Christmas cakes, mince pies and puddings, offer shortbread, home-made sweets done up in fancy boxes or cartons, jams, preserves, pickles and other delicacies wrapped in cellophane packs and embellished with a tinsel ribbon bow.

Make gift tags from old Christmas cards trimmed with pinking shears and threaded with a length of ribbon. Deft fingers can create charming calendars by making tiny arrangements of artificial or dried flowers stuck into plasticine and fixed firmly with fuse wire on to decorative or painted cardboard plates. (See figure 4.) A cheap calendar from the chain stores can be stuck on to the bottom of each plate and a short length of thread pierced through the top, will serve to hang it up.

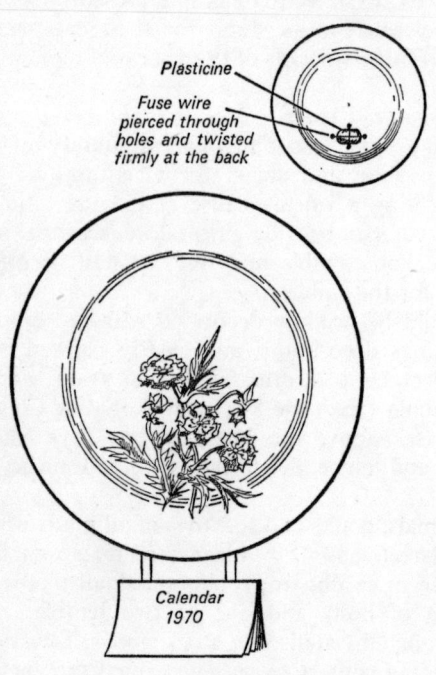

Fig. 4. A Christmas calendar

Sell bunches of freshly picked holly, yew and fir, pine cones collected on summer holidays, ready gilded preserved leaves and flowers and pieces of tree bark. Tins of spray paint bought from the chain stores make this an easy task for those in charge of preparations.

Instructions for fabricating Christmas table arrangements will be found in Chapter 7. Tree decorations can be fashioned from yoghurt cartons and milk bottle tops. Press the latter over a lemon squeezer and trim the edges with scissors, spray with gold or red paint and thread in threes with tinsel ribbon. Yoghurt cartons (the bell shaped variety) only require painting and decorating with a border of tinsel. Large curtain rings, twisted with coloured ribbon or tinsel, pine cones, decorated with glittering paint and given a twist of wire around each base for hanging purposes, will all help to make a large profit from this Yuletide Bonanza Bazaar.

Chapter 6

How children can raise money

Some children are naturally disposed towards fund raising. Whether their interest springs from a genuine desire to help others, or from a passion for watching coins drop into collecting tins, remains in question. But their efforts are invariably crowned with success and I put this down to the naturally appealing manner of children and the fact that they arouse sentiment in others quite unconsciously. Let us hope that by expending time and energy working in this way, they will sow the seeds of virtue and practise similar activity in adult life.

A child's desire to help those less fortunate than himself can be nurtured in a number of ways. If he sees his parents working with determination to raise money for good causes, the chances are that he will be urged to follow suit. The influence of church and school, a talk given by a handicapped person or an authority from a charitable institution can all strike a sympathetic chord in youngsters if the time and circumstances are right.

Nevertheless, there are many inspiring words which fall on stony ground, but don't worry if your children fall into this category. It is fatal to persuade them to do this sort of thing against their will, but be ready in case your child is suddenly fired with enthusiasm for no apparent reason. Give him every assistance and encouragement and advice if it's asked for.

The suggestions described in this chapter have all taken place in private houses and gardens in our small community. However, there is nothing to stop you from moving the proceedings to larger premises. Hire the Church Hall for a Tots to Teens Fashion Show or hold the Lollipop Fair in a large garden.

We have found that friends and neighbours who have supported the children on one occasion will continue to do so at subsequent events and usually ask if they may bring their friends and their children. This makes each project just that much more successful than the previous one. I can assure you that the following functions were enjoyed by us all and the annual events appear to be eagerly anticipated by the public, the participants and, not least, the charity which receives considerable benefit.

Putting on a pantomime

Christmas wouldn't be Christmas in our house without the advent of 'the pantomime'. For as long as I can remember, the few weeks preceding the festive season have been filled with a constant fever of excitement as plans are laid, players cast for their roles and frantic preparations made for clothes, scenery and adapting the musical score.

If you have a family with theatrical aspirations, lots of friends and plenty of energy, help them to organise a Christmas show. Ours has always been a simple homely affair, held in our roomy sitting-room cleared of furniture and filled with borrowed forms and chairs. The children write out about fifty invitations to friends and supporters of their special charity, adding in large letters R.S.V.P. This brings the desired result of a donation even if the recipient is unable to attend.

It is surprising how little effort is needed to get a pantomime going. Start by telling the children to read all the old fairy tale stories to each other. Encourage them to dress up and experiment with the situation and play it out for fun. Before long, you'll find a play taking shape. You'll hear fragments of songs, or a wicked queen asking her mirror, 'Who is the fairest one of all?'

From then onwards, everything moves fast. Offer a few suggestions to the players and urge them to improvise and lengthen each scene. Children are incredibly imaginative and once encouraged blossom in an astonishingly professional manner. One thing leads to another and with gentle and tactful guidance, results will soon begin to show. The important thing to impress upon the children is to come forward and face the front when saying their lines, which must be spoken slowly and clearly. Suggest they include some dancing and also a song or two, inviting the audience to join in.

Of course, complications arise and music can be a headache if you haven't a pianist at hand. Sometimes we've made do with excerpts from records played straight from the gramophone, or taped the music on to a tape recorder from either a gramophone or a pianist. But it is essential to organise the musical side of the show properly and use a theme song to fill in between scenes, cover inevitable gaps, and generally hold the show together.

Take illustrations from books to inspire you with ideas for costumes. Most families have a dressing-up box and once you let it be known in the neighbourhood that clothes are needed for a children's theatrical production, you'll find all manner of garments left on your doorstep. Our loft is crammed with long, full-skirted evening gowns, battered garden party hats and discarded bridesmaids' dresses, which serve to robe queens, princesses and ugly sisters in magnificent style. Old sheets can be dyed and cut up for dwarfs' tunics, a king's robe or a witch's cloak. The mounting excitement as children see themselves transformed into fairytale characters is reward enough for the mothers who cut up, sew and adapt the styles from the pictures, with the help of any existing dress patterns they may happen to have. Books giving instructions are available to help. *Costumes for School Plays* by Barbara Snook, published by Batsford (16s.), is invaluable. Instructions for making hats, shoes and accessories are included as well.

Although a pantomime is satisfactory because of its strong, meaty plot, there are plenty of other ways of entertaining which children may prefer. Burlesques, humorous songs and sketches, short one act plays and potted pantomimes can be obtained for a few shillings from the Keith Prowse Music Publishing Company (address page 104). Plays will be sent on approval and advice given on the type of entertainment most suitable for the company by writing to H. F. W. Deane and Sons Ltd (address page 101).

Other textbooks which would help any show along are:

Textbook on Stagecraft by Susan Richmond, price 5s., available H. F. W. Deane.
Guide to Greasepaint published by Samuel French, price 2s. 6d. address page 102).
Youth Club Skits and Stunts by Sid Hedges, published by (Methuen, price 12s. 6d.

A tots-to-teens fashion show

At our Mannequin Parade held some years ago, the response was so overwhelming that the show had to be repeated at a later date. The models comprised seven girls whose ages ranged from six to sixteen and two small boys who lapped up the atmosphere of this rather feminine affair and added enormously to its success.

Nobody bought any special new clothes for this event at all. A vast supply of every conceivable type of garment, from beach togs to swinging pop clothes, poured out of the children's and friends' wardrobes, in an unending stream. The difficulty lay in having to chose from them.

It was an enchanting spectacle to watch these innocents parading down the centre of a neighbour's large 'through' room, sometimes arrayed in angelic smocked party frills, or clad in dungarees and check shirts for play, and finally presenting a goodnight parade of slumberwear, with a rumpled four-year-old male model in nightshirt and nightcap. I remember the profits surprised everybody and spurred the children on to further money-raising efforts in the future.

If you plan to run a similar show, remember that several mothers will be needed to help off-stage with changing clothes. An older child must compère and hold the show together. Soft music should be played in the background. The idea can be extended by the children singing appropriate nursery rhymes, dancing or miming to music when the clothes suggest it.

Carol singing

Very little encouragement is needed to persuade children to sing carols before Christmas, but do see they are well rehearsed before allowing them to plague the neighbours. If any of the children can play the recorder or some other instrument, this improves the performance enormously and bumps up the profits. Children under sixteen are not allowed to collect money in the street, so an adult should accompany them.

A most touching and moving spectacle took place in a corner of our market square at the height of the shopping spree just before Christmas one year. A group of Catholic schoolchildren formed a tableau of the Nativity, whilst others clustered round them singing the well-known carols. The incredible sum of £43 was collected in just over half-an-hour!

This charming idea could be carried out by as few as three children, with an adult in charge of the collection. Ensure that the position taken up by the singers does not cause congestion of traffic or pedestrians.

A lollipop fair

A summer event with the above title offers a stimulating challenge to children. The long holidays can be put to useful and profitable purpose planning this special function which is directed mainly at young people. At the same time stalls can be stocked with sufficiently saleable items in order to attract parents and other adults as well.

The children make a start by canvassing friends, neighbours and supporters for surplus garden produce, items of cookery, white elephants, books, records and so on. This means writing out advance notices, collecting the goods offered and extracting a donation or promises from benefactors to turn up on the day of the event. See that the children play their part too, by encouraging the older ones to bake sweets and other simple recipes within their capabilities. Others can look out their discarded toys, books, clothes and records. A raffle cake, baked in the shape of a lollipop will bring in some extra shillings.

Present every child attending under the age of sixteen with a free lollipop and make a special effort to provide swings, a climbing frame, a slide and any large mechanical toys which small children would enjoy. Charge a penny or twopence for a ride or a limited amount of play. A kitchen minute timer is useful here.

Run a 'Nosh up' stall selling pop-corn, biscuits, sweets, gingerbread men, sausages on sticks and chocolate kisses. Quench the thirst of competitors with glasses of home-made lemon or orange squash.

The following sideshows are particularly suited to children's functions and details on how to set them up can be found in Chapter 8:

Catch a fish.
Candle snuffing with water pistols.
Darts with a difference.
Cover the silver pieces.
Knock off the hat.

Bucket ball.
Treasure hunt.

An extremely popular stall is called 'The Dressing Up Stall'. This consists of suitable items for children, sifted from collected jumble. Small girls are enthralled with almost anything from old costume jewellery, outmoded shoes to a bridal outfit. And what boy wouldn't enjoy buying a deer-stalker hat or an ancient battledress?

A wildly successful project for an occasion like this is to provide a 'Chamber of Horrors'. This can be rigged up in a tent, garage or out-house with enormous spine-chilling effect.

Darkness is essential and the only lighting required is a torch. A record playing 'Haunted House Mystery Sounds and Music' (Castle HMX 1) helps to establish the eerie atmosphere as each child is guided by a ghost through a series of horrific experiences. For instance:

1. A dish of peeled grapes presented as a dead man's eyes.
2. A rubber glove filled with flour as a hand.
3. A dried prune as an ear.
4. A mask (appropriately splashed with red paint or tomato ketchup to simulate blood) stuffed with newspaper and covered with a wig and suspended by thread from the roof. A beam of light from the torch flickers briefly across this gruesome sight, which is, of course, meant to represent a dead man's head.
5. Strands of suspended wool brushing across the faces of spectators as they pass from one exhibit to the next, giving the sensation of walking through cobwebs.

I have no doubt that many other gory ideas can be added to this list by boys and girls with a lurid imagination.

The afternoon's activities reach their climax with the advent of 'The Lollipop Races'. This simply means that winners receive lollipops as prizes, which should be of a slightly more elaborate nature than those offered on admission. (Chain stores and sweet shops offer plenty of variety.) The following list gives the good old favourite competitions which go down best.

Three-legged race.
Egg and spoon race.

68 How children can raise money

Sack race.
Slow bicycle race.
Statues.
Wheelbarrow race.
Piggyback race.
Obstacle race.
Relay races.
Flower pot contest. (Provide two rows of staggered flower pots placed upside-down and a pair of binoculars. The competitor who can step along the flower pots, looking through a pair of binoculars reversed without putting a foot on the ground, is the winner.)

If it is possible to obtain the services of a magician this would be a welcome added attraction. Alternatively, the children themselves could put on a puppet show. The children's librarian at your public library would be pleased to supply informative books.

A competition for the best picture of 'My Mum' would create a great deal of amusement and interest for the spectators. Provide paper and pencils and somewhere to pin up the results and judge the favourite by asking everybody to place a penny beneath the drawing of their choice.

Individual efforts

When I asked my children if they could think of any other ways in which they could raise money, the answer came, 'Well, there are all the awful things like washing cars and cutting the lawns'.

Here, for the benefit of those admirable families whose younger members prefer to raise cash the hard way, I have listed some tried and tested methods used successfully by local schoolchildren to make money for a school project during the holidays.

Shoe cleaning.
Wood chopping.
Clothes washing.
Ironing.
Baby-sitting.
Making Christmas cards.
Cooking toffee and toffee apples.
Cutting lawns.

How children can raise money 69

Cutting hedges.
Sweeping up the snow.
Running errands.
Fruit-picking.
Sweeping up the leaves.
Collecting 'empties' after social events, and returning them to licensed houses.
Washing paintwork.
Cleaning silver.
Cleaning windows.
Clearing out an attic or garage.
Distempering outhouses.
Taking dogs for walks.
Car washing.

Chapter 7

What to make, sell and sew

As the date of the fête, bazaar or sale of work approaches, a mounting sense of panic frequently takes hold of the organisers. What items can be offered for sale? Are there any fresh, quick and easy ideas for articles to make and for displaying them.

Methods for collecting money and merchandise

The first essential is for money to be collected months beforehand, so that merchandise can either be bought for re-sale at a profit, or the money used for buying materials so that articles can be made by those with the time and skill to produce them.

Talents projects

Coffee mornings (see page 31) can raise cash for this purpose, but there is another popular method known as 'The Talents Project' which works in the following manner. Supporters of the cause are given 2s. 6d. or 5s. and asked to invest it according to the talents of each person.

A generous, but definite period of time should be stated so that the most profit can be extracted from the original sum. Naturally, there are a multitude of ways in which the money can be used to bring forth the desired result, but here is a list of how others have tackled the challenge. It should be pointed out, that the small profit made in the first instance by selling the article made should be re-invested as many times as possible.

Buy:
An ounce of wool to knit a pair of baby's bootees.
A yard of gingham to make an apron or table mats.
Ingredients to bake cakes, make sweets, pastries, etc.
A packet of seeds to grow seedlings.
Cartridge paper to paint birthday cards or notelets.
A frame and material to make a lampshade.
A small doll to dress.

A piece of felt and filling to create a soft toy.
Club together with others and hold a sherry morning.
Doubtless there are many more ideas which are not mentioned, particularly in the field of garden produce. But everybody has some creative ability and this is the time to reveal it.

Jumble and how to sort it

Other methods for procuring merchandise for your Sale include asking for gifts and donations (see page 12), contacting the Art Department of your local College of Further Education for throw-outs of paintings, pottery and sculpture and by nagging everybody you know to turn out their attics, garages, sheds and cupboards to give you anything they can spare.

Whoever undertakes to canvass, collect and sift the fearful assortment of garments, objects and sheer junk which is given for good causes, deserves the undying gratitude of the organiser. This project lies at the very heart of all sales in aid of charity and those with experience know full well that the rewards are great if sufficient time and trouble are given to sorting items over and over again.

Stalls

Use imagination and enterprise to offer the goods for sale on appropriate stalls, e.g.:

Any clothes in mint condition put on the 'Good as New' stall.
Sell trinkets, jewellery, bric-a-brac, etc. from a stall captioned 'Objets d'Art'.
Sell discarded records from 'Collector's Corner'.
Books can be arranged on shelves labelled 'Books for Browsers'.
Offer household articles of any size at the 'White Elephant' stall.

Display and staging of goods

Clothes must be separated into men's and women's sections. Hang up dresses and suits on an improvised rack (dry cleaners or dress shops may be willing to lend you one) and jumpers, shoes, hats, skirts and blouses, too, need to be put in special piles and marked with the prices clearly. It is a great advantage if all the items in each box cost the same amount.

Be on your guard to spot the occasional article which might be of value. A reputable shopkeeper selling similar merchandise will be willing to tell you approximately what it is worth. Certain items such as picture frames or jewellery may fetch a better price if sold to a dealer. Use imagination and explore every possible channel to ensure you get the best price for each item. If you're unable to get the figure you know an article to be worth, don't let it go for a song – there is usually another function coming up when it will fetch the right price.

I need hardly enlarge upon the remaining stalls which have become an established pattern at fêtes and bazaars everywhere. The *cake stall* has come to be interpreted loosely and covers absolutely any item of home-baked cooking which can be transported home by customers. At the *garden produce stall* plants, cut flowers, fruit and vegetables are collected and sold in quantity. The *handicraft stall* speaks for itself, while the *toy stall* offers hand-made animals, gonks, dolls and other toys. A *gift stall* displays oddments such as pomanders, pot-pourri, hand painted china, stone paper-weights and anything else suitable for a present. A *tombola stall* (see page 89) and a *raffle* (see page 14) complete the list, but turn to Chapters 2, 5 and 8 where you will find many more suggestions.

Assuming you have collected a large amount of all manner of items to sell, how are you going to set about displaying them in an attractive manner? This does call for considerable forethought and is indeed a subject in its own right. Much can be learnt from reading books on window display and I can recommend *Window Dressing* by G. Faziakerley, published by English Universities Press (7s. 6d.).

To touch briefly upon this important matter, do ascertain that the type of merchandise offered for sale is advertised clearly for all to see. Try to enlist the help of a handyman to erect a framework over your stall. If this is not possible, improvise with two long bamboo poles, placed in pails of earth, one either side of the stall (see figure 5). This structure is strong enough to support a width of shelf paper secured to either pole with sticky tape. As well as depicting the articles for sale in large letters, paint a rag doll if it's a toy stall, draw mothers to the babywear display with a cut-out stork and illustrate the home baked cooking stall with a wooden spoon and a birthday cake.

The staging of goods too is vital. Place items worthy of note on upturned painted boxes, tins, or in the case of lightweight articles, on columns of corrugated paper.

Easy articles to make and sew

Finally, here are a few suggestions for articles to make. I have purposely left out the more commonplace handicrafts, such as knitted garments and the obvious sewing notions as much written information is available in books and journals on these subjects.

Fig. 5. A simple method for erecting a frame over a stall

Instead I have selected a few slightly off-beat ideas, which I have made myself and know to be easy sellers. None requires skill, only patience and a little perseverance, and all can be made quickly and inexpensively. Do not expect a monetary reward for the labour you expend on producing these items. This is your contribution to your cause and providing you cover expenses, and make a small profit you should be well satisfied.

Hand painted personal mugs

Buy a number of cheap, plain mugs from the chain stores or rejects from china shops and distinguish each by painting a child's name boldly across the centre. Choose the more common names like JOHN, SARAH, PETER or ANN. Vertical lines around the rest of the mug enhance the result, but are not essential. Orders can be

74 What to make, sell and sew

taken for later delivery if the right name is not available on the day of the Sale.

Use red or blue Tri-Chem paint tubes which cost 3s. 11d. each and are obtainable from Selfridges (address page 104). As painting is done straight from the tube on to the mug, no brush is necessary. It is then baked in the oven which renders it completely washable.

Pomanders

Enchanting clove oranges, used in olden times to ward off 'evil odours' and now hung in wardrobes or anywhere in the house as a sweet smelling decoration.

Use thick skinned ripe oranges and stud with cloves (one 7d. packet is enough to cover three). Wrap in tissue paper and put in a dark cupboard for a couple of weeks. When thoroughly

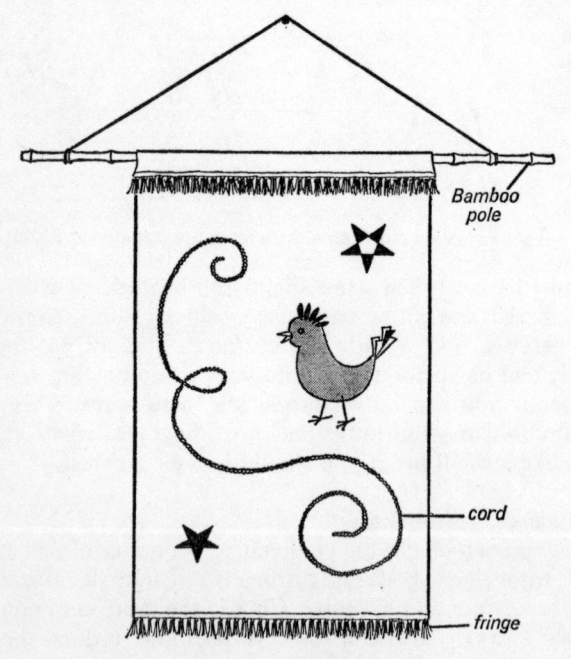

Fig. 6. A banner

What to make, sell and sew

dry, press a staple into the top of each orange, threading a yard of ribbon to hang the pomander where required.

Banners

These gay, colourful wall hangings are easily fabricated from lengths of felt which has the tremendous advantage that it does not fray and therefore requires no hemming. Simply cut a piece approximately 25 by 12 inches. Make a 1-inch hem at the top, thread a piece of bamboo stick through this and attach thin cord at each end ready for hanging (see figure 6).

Decorations on the banner can be made from smaller pieces of felt of different colours cut out to make one of the following pictures or themes. Nursery rhyme figures can be traced from book illustrations and used as a guide to cut the figures or shapes and sewn or stuck on to the banner with cow-gum. A set of four small banners could depict the Seasons – a robin on a fir tree with a background of snow for Winter, lambs and crocuses for Spring, butterflies, flowers and sun for Summer and harvest fruits for Autumn. But simple, gay, pop-art shapes in flowers and leaves look extremely effective and require less effort.

Book markers

Save old envelopes and cut the clean corners diagonally, varying the edges slightly. (See figure 7.) These markers are used to slip

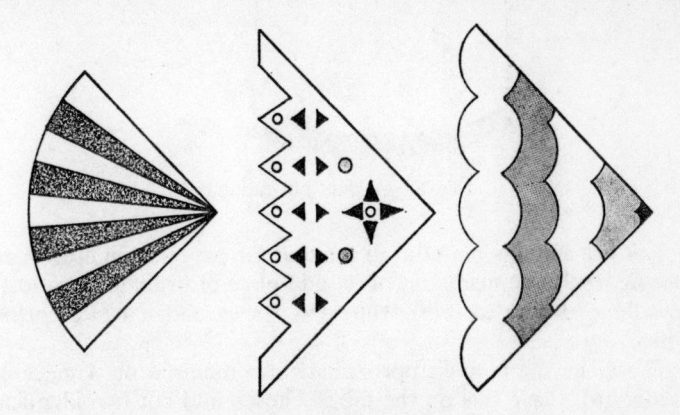

Fig. 7. Book markers

over the corner of book pages. Paint horizontal or vertical stripes, dots or any imaginative design. Sell for 1d., 2d. or 3d. according to your public. These are simple enough for children to make.

Giant pin cushions

These create a stir wherever they appear and make most acceptable gifts at Christmas time, as well as serving a practical purpose throughout the year.

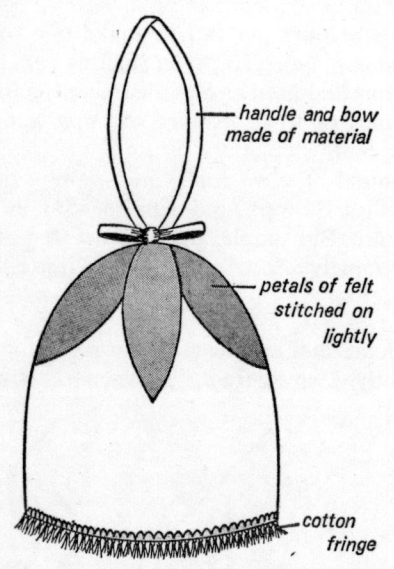

Fig. 8. A giant pin cushion

Felt is a suitable material to use, but the pin cushion illustrated (see figure 8) was made out of an odd piece of brilliant, turquoise towelling, decorated with white felt leaves and a white cotton fringe.

Draw the shape and approximate size required on a piece of cardboard. Place this on the fabric chosen and cut two identical pieces ¾ inch larger all round. Machine the two sides together, leaving the bottom end open. Turn to the right side. Insert the cardboard and fill up either side with kapok packed very firmly to form a padded cushion.

You will now be left with a rounded open base. Turn the edges of the material in, cover with another piece cut to size, and neatly hem in position.

Add the final decorative touches by stitching on felt leaves and making a handle and bow, either by using the same material or a yard of ribbon. Tack a length of cotton fringe around the bottom to neaten the base.

Stone paperweights
Wash and dry large stones thoroughly. Cover with ordinary household glossy paint in bright colours and when bone dry, embellish by painting with dots, zig-zags, squiggles or flower shapes in contrasting colours. A final coat of clear varnish gives a professional finish.

Sequin ear-rings
Attract teenagers with these simply made glittering drop ear-rings. The only requirements are large sequins with holes top and bottom, ear-ring mounts, fuse wire and a touch of Araldite glue.

Construct by threading the individual sequins together, one below the other. Three for each ear-ring looks effective. Twist the wire neatly behind each sequin and trim the ends short with scissors. Fix on to the mount with a touch of glue and leave overnight to set. Small flat buttons without centre holes make attractive ear-rings too. Stick them on to the mounts in the same way.

Sequins in glorious colours and ear-ring mounts are available for a shilling or so from Bourne and Hollingsworth (address page 101).

A Christmas table centre
Distinctive arrangements for the table, mantelpiece or hall add a flourish to the Festive Season. A simple decoration can be made with the following materials, but do adapt and substitute anything suitable you may have in hand.

On to a round cake board, empty a half packet of 'Polyfilla'

78 What to make, sell and sew

mixed to the consistency of fairly stiff porridge. Place in the centre a large red candle and three scallop shells from your fishmonger. These look most attractive painted gold or silver. Round this centrepiece, insert an assortment of gilded ferns, holly, ivy and tiny poinsettias bought from the chain stores. Alternatively, dried flowers and leaves can be prepared and painted gold or silver and used in the same manner. Small cones can be pierced with a stub wire or cocktail stick and added for general effect, as can red ribbon bows, baubles and Christmas bells (see figure 9).

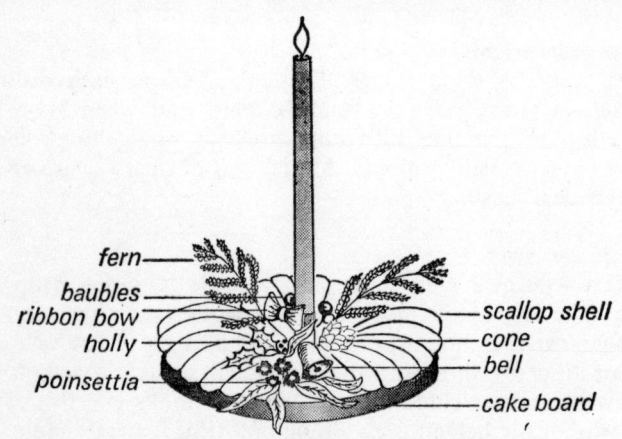

Fig. 9. A Christmas table centre

Decorative Christmas crackers

These will enchant both young and old and can be used as table centres, as gifts, or pinned to the front door as a welcome to your guests.

The cracker is fashioned from a yard of 54-inch net, a 7-inch length of cylindrical cardboard (the discarded roll of silver foil wrapping paper is ideal), some elastic bands and a few tiny, gilded, dried flowers or one or two small, sparkling decorations bought at the chain stores.

Cover the 7-inch tube with a piece of silver foil, cut a 1-inch hole in the centre and fill with a little 'Oasis' (obtainable from the florists). Fold the net into four and cut, so that you have four pieces of equal size (18 by 26 inches). Roll one of these round the tube and fix at each end with an elastic band (see figure 10a). Cut the remaining three pieces of net in half, thereby making six pieces (9 by 26 inches), and gather one up by hand in concertina fashion, placing an elastic band in the middle (see figure

A — a cylindrical roll covered in foil and net, elastic band, hole filled with oasis

B — gather the remaining six strips of net into a frill

C — place three on each end of the cracker, secured by elastic bands

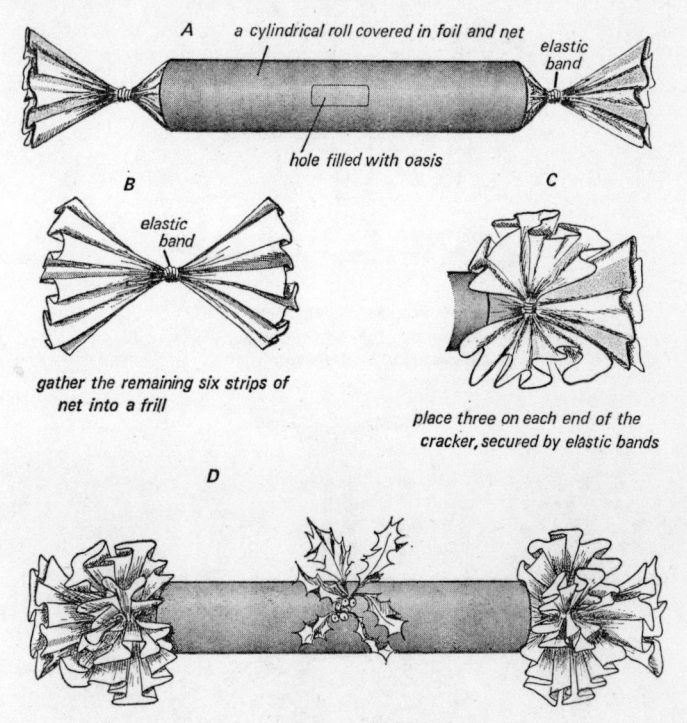

D

Fig. 10. Decorative Christmas crackers

10b). Repeat this with the remaining five pieces and place three on each end of the cracker with elastic bands (see figure 10c). Place your flowers in the small centre square (see figure 10d).

A bath puff

This elegant confection of net is designed to take the place of the soggy cleaning rag in most bathrooms. It is a remarkable nylon

80 What to make, sell and sew

net ball which remains crisp and efficient for the task for a considerable length of time.

From ½ yard of 54-inch nylon net, cut three strips 6 inches

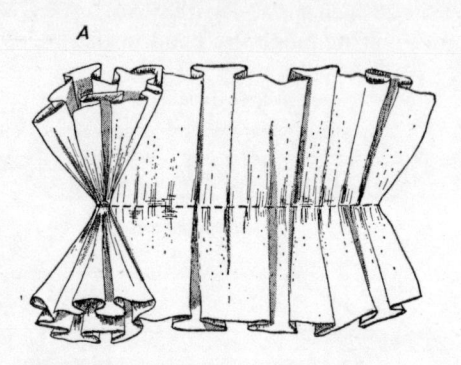

Roll the first strip of gathered net into a ball. Place the second strip round the outside of the first and finally add the third strip

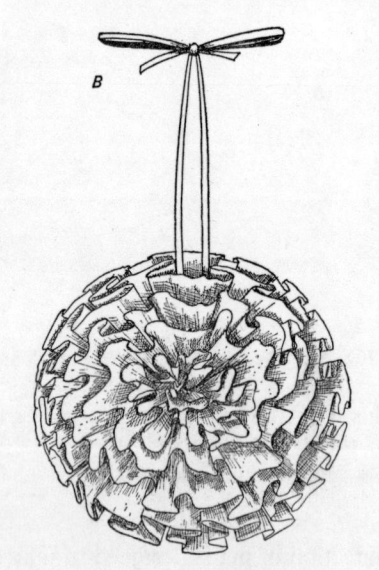

Fig. 11. A Bath puff

wide. If you have a sewing machine, adjust it to make a long stitch, and machine down the centre of each strip, otherwise run a gathering thread by hand. Pull each thread and gather tightly, rolling the first one along the gathered thread (see figure 11a). Place the second strip round the outside of the first and finally add the third strip, gathering each one as tightly as possible. Tie a yard of ribbon round the centre of the last length of net and pull the ends, knotting firmly. Frill out the net to produce a fluffy ball and leave the ends of the ribbon to make a loop so that the ball can be hung for speedy drying after use (see figure 11b).

Brass rubbings

In the last few years, mediaeval engravings of bishops, knights, ladies and monks have become immensely fashionable for home decoration. Impressions of these figures, which can be found in many churches, can be taken on paper by rubbing with heelball wax. The results make extremely striking wall hangings. Many churches possess fine brasses, but be sure to obtain permission from the vicar or verger beforehand and it is usual to offer him a small donation towards the church funds.

You will require a roll of shelfpaper, a stick of heelball wax (obtainable from shoe repairers or art shops), sticky tape and a soft rag or brush for sweeping the brass clean before beginning work.

Place the paper over the figure and secure the four edges with sticky tape. Rub with the heelball, starting from the top and working downwards – a fairly tedious task. The amount of pressure used determines the depth of darkness of the result.

Rubbings can be mounted by cutting out the figures carefully, sticking the edges with cow-gum and placing on large sheets of good quality white or grey art paper. A more impressive effect can be obtained by using cheap hessian. Different coloured rubbings can be achieved with special wax crayons. These, and all brass rubbing requisites can be purchased from Phillips and Page (address page 103).

Decorated wooden spoons

For a splash of colour on the kitchen wall, provide a galaxy of gaudy and colourfully painted wooden spoons.

Paint plain wooden spoons with red, emerald green, royal blue glossy paint or poster colours. When dry, paint ornamental designs in contrasting colours. Stripes, stars and dots look particularly effective. A final overall coat of varnish if you use poster paints will give a shine to the finished object.

Faces, too, can be painted on to the back of these spoons and surrounded with yellow wool to simulate hair. Fix this on with glue. Hooks must be screwed in neatly for hanging the spoons the right way up.

A paper serviette apron

The last idea I have to offer in this selection of things to make is merely a gimmick. However, it is amusing to create and quick to sell.

Take half a dozen large, strong paper napkins and stitch them on to a 1½ inch band of strong material or a length of webbing. The point of this is, that when worn, the top layer can be used to wipe sticky fingers, and torn off and discarded when dirty.

Chapter 8

Sideshows, contests and other attractions

'Bowling for the Pig', 'Coconut Shies' and other similar novelties held at summer fêtes are an accepted part of the British way of life. The public expects to find such amusements on these occasions and would be extremely disappointed if they were missing. With a little ingenuity and forethought, a good deal of money can be raised by putting on a number of sideshows, a contest or two, combined with a variety of captivating attractions.

Much will depend on the talents of your committee and their families. The husband of a Women's Institute member I know has constructed the money-spinner – 'Penny on the Square' from a trestle table base, with a special hardboard top painted with squares, complete with four chutes for rolling the pennies. Elaborate methods for tipping glamorous females out of bed and testing a competitor's strength can also be fabricated successfully by enthusiastic handymen.

Unfortunately, we cannot afford to rely on these clever people. If, as so often happens, it is left to the women of the community to organise the side-shows, the ideas must be simple and straightforward. All my suggestions, therefore, can be made without much difficulty and require very little in the way of props. Everything should be borrowed and set up in position as early as possible on the day of the event and considerable thought given to the lay-out. Devise a plan to ensure that customers flow easily from one attraction to another. Place the refreshments at the furthest point from the entrance so that all the stalls and sideshows will be passed en route. If the site permits, place these in a large circle, leaving the central space free for contests, events and other entertainments.

Sideshows

In the suggestions described I have deliberately omitted stating a figure for the entrance fee. This can only be decided by trial and error, depending on the age, financial status and the ability of your competitors. Your best plan will be to try your sideshow out on some of the helpers. Your aim should be to distribute about 1s. in prizes for every 1s. 6d. or 2s. collected. This will encourage people to enter again and again. It is sometimes appropriate to fix a different price for children and adults or for men and women.

Prizes awarded can be small trinkets, handkerchiefs, bars of chocolate, packets of seeds, sweets, biscuits, pencils and other inexpensive and acceptable items. If wrapped in colourful paper, these will bring enormous pleasure to recipients and encourage them to spend more. For large functions, wholesale gifts at all prices for both children and adults can be obtained from Barnum's (address page 101).

A treasure hunt

An area of land approximately 12 feet square is roped off. Choose an imaginary spot where the treasure is buried by measuring from the sides with a tape measure. Seal these figures in an envelope beforehand and sell stakes or skewers with the buyers' names inscribed on small attached tickets. If the event is held indoors, a map can be substituted mounted on soft board using pins instead of stakes. Announce the prize towards the end of the afternoon.

China smashing

China shops are often willing to give away broken and chipped crockery to help raise money for charity, but make your requests early in the year. Ideally, the china should be placed on shelves against a background of strong tarpaulin or a brick wall. No prizes need be offered, the satisfaction of hurling balls and creating havoc and destruction is sufficient reward. Bashing up an old piano also comes into this category if one is available for demolition.

Bucket ball

Place six buckets in a row, tilted forward at an angle. Give customers old tennis balls and stand them at a distance of 10 feet. Balls thrown must remain in the buckets to win.

Sideshows, contests and other attractions 85

Skittles
Borrow a set of large skittles and set out a throw of about 15 feet with canvas at the back and some way up the sides. Three balls are allowed and a prize awarded if all the skittles are knocked over. Alternatively, a friendly publican may lend you table skittles.

Hoopla laundry
Erect a washing line about 12 feet long pegged with a selection of humorous garments. A pair of long pants, a nappy, some old-fashioned corsets and so on. Provide customers with rings (these can be made from strong wire), and make it clear that both pegs of a garment must be ringed to win a prize.

Ringing the bottle
Place a dozen bottles in a 10-feet square roped-off enclosure. Prepare a few 2-feet lengths of bamboo by attaching a piece of string with a ring tied to the end. Customers stand outside the enclosure and try to ring the bottle necks. (Make sure the rings only just fit.) Allow a time limit of one minute and a prize to whoever 'rings' the most.

Light the candles
This is only suitable for an indoor function. Place candles upright in rows of four on an old piece of board. The competitor endeavours to light as many candles as possible with one match. If he lights six rows with one match, he wins 3d. Nine rows will win him 6d. and eleven – a prize.

Candle snuffing
Although this is more satisfactory if played indoors, it can be erected outside if the lighted candles are placed in a sheltered position.
The idea is for the competitor to take aim with a water pistol and endeavour to extinguish as many lighted candle flames with one 'shot' of water as possible. The line behind which he must stand in order to perform this feat and the prize offered will have to be worked out according to the size and power of the pistol.

Candles should be easily removable from the candlesticks so that the water can be shaken off and the candle re-lit while held on its side.

Darts with a difference

More popular than the usual dartboard, this idea has proved very attractive with the young. Rope off a 12-feet square and place a couple of dozen folded paper bags containing varying amounts of money on the ground. Leave some of the bags empty, but in the others put pennies and larger sums of money. Competitors must pierce the paper bag with a dart in order to win the contents.

Cover the silver pieces

Provide a large shallow tub of water with several 6d. pieces and one or two florins on the bottom. Anybody who can successfully cover one of the silver coins by dropping a penny and covering it completely wins the silver piece.

Electric bell ringer

Although this may sound complicated, I understand that it is simple enough for most teenage schoolboys to construct in a jiffy. Certainly it attracts young and old to try their luck. Buy a battery operated electric bell, a 4 feet length of $\frac{1}{4}$-inch copper pipe and a piece of $\frac{1}{8}$-inch brass rod, 1 foot long, and some insulated electric wire. A wooden stand is made out of two lengths of 2 × 2 wood fixed to a base with shelf brackets. The copper pipe is bent into a snake-like shape and fixed between the two uprights of the stand. Connect one wire to this pipe and to one side of the bell. Fix the other side of the bell with a piece of flex to the brass rod. Bend the other end of the rod into a ring about one inch in diameter and pass it over the copper pipe. Cover one inch of the bent pipe at each end with insulating tape. The competitor holds the brass rod and carefully manoeuvres it along the bent copper pipe from one end to the other, without making contact. If he touches the pipe, the bell will ring and he loses the game. If he is successful he wins a small prize.

Knock off the hat

I gather from my children that the outstanding sideshow of their lives was trying to knock off a man's top hat with tennis balls.

Sideshows, contests and other attractions

A large hardboard screen is erected which protects and covers a live man from his knees to the top of his head. The victim stalks up and down wearing a top hat which projects above the screen and competitors aim to knock it off with the balls while he is moving.

Catch a fish

Small children will be fascinated by this fishing competition. A large bowl is filled with water which looks more attractive if coloured blue with ink. A dozen small metal fish can be made by cutting out shapes from old tins (or substitute metal bottle tops).

The competition is to catch all the fish in a certain time, using a 2-feet stick with a piece of string to which is attached a small magnet.

Contests

Apart from the usual sideshows and entertainments try to provide a couple of contests to add an element of excitement to the occasion. Although there are a number of ideas for these and other attractions throughout the book, to assist readers, I have compiled a list which includes these, as well as giving further suggestions.

A beauty contest

Advertise well ahead and ask shops to display posters and distribute entry forms to attract competitors.

In most contests, the girls begin by walking in single file, so that the judges get an overall impression. Afterwards, they appear individually, when marks are awarded for such attributes as figure, face, poise and personality. Make it clear whether summer dresses or swimsuits are to be worn. Remember to provide a room with as many mirrors as possible.

Suitable people to judge are ex-beauty or carnival queens, principals of dancing or drama schools or beauticians from department stores.

A baby show

I am not very happy about recommending this event as much heartache can be caused by the judge's agonising choice of the winner. However, if there is a demand for a show go ahead and organise the event (see above for advance planning) but divide the entries into age groups. Under six months, six months to a year, and so on. Make it clear that the decision of the judges is final. Ask matrons of maternity homes, midwives, health visitors or hospital sisters to perform this task.

A dog show
This is fun for the children and shouldn't be taken too seriously. Follow instructions for the Beauty Contest with regard to advance planning and if you get a large number of entries, divide the animals into appropriate classes according to the type and breed. Otherwise just give prizes for the best groomed dog, the most obedient or the most appealing. A veterinary surgeon, a kennel proprietor or a dog-breeder would make excellent judges.

Other suggestions for contests can include:

The Most Glamorous Grandmother.
The Best Decorated Pram and Owner.
The Most Shapely Ankles.
The Most Elaborate Hair-do.
Bursting Balloons.
Drinking Milk from a baby's bottle (adult males only).
The Knobbliest Knees.

Guessing competitions

Then there are the simple guessing competitions, such as:

The weight of a cake.
The number of beans in a glass jar.
The number of sweets contained in a glass jar.
The number of matches inside a large matchbox.
The name of a doll.
Predicting the time a watch will stop. This is known as a Watch-Stopping Competition and is run in the following manner.

Buy a watch with a second hand from a reliable local jeweller. Sell tickets with the estimated time at which the watch will stop in hours, minutes and seconds. This competition is hedged round with legal restrictions but special printed tickets are worded in

Sideshows, contests and other attractions 89

such a way as to conform with the law. These can be obtained if ordered well in advance from Barnum's (address page 101).

Other attractions

Tombola

This most popular and biggest fund raiser of all time can be run with enormous profit at almost any type of charity function. Begin by begging all your friends to give you a gift of some kind—anything is acceptable from a bottle of champagne down to a packet of pins. When as many items as possible have been collected, number each one with a ticket torn from a book of cloakroom tickets obtainable from stationer's shops. (These can be bought in various colours to avoid confusion.) The corresponding number is placed in a large box and each customer pays 6d., 1s. or even 2s. 6d. for a ticket. The number he draws entitles him to claim the corresponding numbered gift.

How much to charge for a ticket depends on the quality of the items offered and also whether you decide to have some blank numbers, in which case some competitors receive no gifts.

A handkerchief tombola with lucky numbers

This is a slight variation on the above, the difference being that every gift is a handkerchief. Tuck a note saying 'Lucky Number' inside a few of the handkerchiefs and award a small extra prize when these numbers are drawn. If you can secure the handkerchiefs on to an upright display board, this competition will attract considerably more attention.

Hydrogen balloons

Balloons filled with hydrogen gas, each one carrying a specially printed postcard are released on the ground for a charge of 1s. to the competitor. The card bears the printed name and address of the organiser to whom the card is to be returned when found. On the other side is printing to the effect that a prize will be awarded to the sender of the balloon which travels the greatest distance, as well as to the finder who returns the winning balloon card (the one found at the greatest distance from the place of release). A definite date should be stated on which the winning competitor is to be declared. This is usually fixed at approximately three weeks from the day of the Fête.

The cost works out at about 4½d. for each balloon released for large quantities, and slightly more for smaller numbers. Full details of the hire of cylinders, the cost of balloons, postcards and twine are available from Barnum's (address page 101).

Pony rides

Contact local riding schools in your neighbourhood and children who own sturdy, good-tempered ponies. Detail a reliable adult experienced with horses to keep an eye on the proceedings and see that all goes well.

A pneumatic drill

Have you always longed to try your hand at working one of these fearful machines? A local firm of contractors willingly supplied one free of charge for the afternoon of our fête! An operator came along too and collected 6d. a head from eager would-be roadmenders.

Trampoline

It is sometimes possible to borrow one of these from nearby Air Force stations or Physical Education Training Centres. If you've seen one in use at any other functions in your neighbourhood, find out where and how they borrowed it by contacting the organisers.

Fried chips

This marvellous idea is practised regularly by a large school I know, in order to raise money for their various projects.

The hardest chore of this undertaking is the unsavoury task of peeling the potatoes, but once this has been accomplished, the going is easy. A couple of picnic stoves are adequate if mains gas or electricity is not available. Apart from two saucepans of fat, the potatoes and a supply of greaseproof paper bags, the whole enterprise is almost sheer profit. It's certain that at 6d. a packet, you'll run out of potatoes, bags and energy long before the demand is satisfied.

Portrait sketches

If there is an artist living in your district capable of producing quick portrait sketches bearing a moderate resemblance to their sitters, ask if he would offer his talents to benefit your Cause. Try to provide a secluded corner where the sitting can take place and keep the fee fairly low, say 5s. for a small sketch about 4 × 6 inches. Silhouettes are popular too if you know of anybody who has mastered the art of quick on-the-spot portraits in profile.

Entertainments

Finally, here are suggestions for entertainments and attractions for which the public will not necessarily be charged extra. The advantage of staging shows and mounting exhibitions lies entirely in the added inducement offered to people to come along and enjoy themselves. Once inside they're bound to spend money on something.

There are several ways to track down organisers of the associations listed below. Enquire at your library and Citizens' Advice Bureau, search through local classified telephone directories, town directories and newspapers. Under the heading 'Entertainments' in the latter, you will find not only magicians and conjurors, but you may discover more unusual and exciting performers who will add fun and zest to your function.

DANCING

Children's Dancing
Folk Dancing
Morris Dancing
National Dancing
Highland Dancing

MUSIC

Bell Ringing
Accordion Playing
Girls' Choirs
Male Voice Choirs
Madrigal Singers

Operatic Singers
Brass Bands
Pipers
Orchestras, etc.

PHYSICAL EDUCATION AND SPORT

Judo
Karate
Weight Lifting
Horsemanship

Ladies' Keep Fit
Gymnastics
Archery
Fencing

92 Sideshows, contests and other attractions

The following Services can be approached to help with various of the above demonstrations or provide others:

Army	St. John Ambulance Brigade
Navy	Girls' Life Brigade
Air Force	Boys' Brigade
Police	Sea Cadets
Fire Brigade	Scouts and Guides

EXHIBITIONS	THEATRICAL ENTERTAINMENTS, ETC.
Art	Punch and Judy
Photography	Puppet Shows
Model Railways	Conjurors
Floral Displays	Clowns
Horticulture	Magicians
Handicrafts of all kinds	Film Shows
	Mannequin Parades
	Millinery Parades

Chapter 9

How national charities raise money

How do the big charities like Oxfam, the Spastics Society, Save the Children Fund and others raise such fantastic sums of money? When we read of their achievements in this field we can only marvel at the scope and variety of their successful projects.

These large societies, however, do start with two distinct advantages. Many of them employ full-time professionally trained men and women to organise this important part of their work and almost without exception, their headquarters are in London where they have access to all the resources of that great city. Nevertheless, if you think back to the early times of these societies, when they were practically unknown, you will soon realise that their key word was, and still is, 'publicity'. These people know that the money they spend on advertising will repay them over and over again.

Apart from making their aims and purposes known to the public by this method, you will notice that many of their fund raising projects such as appeals, charity balls, film premières and similar large functions are given enormous publicity too. To make known a forthcoming event various news items may be used. For instance:

1. The Mayor issues a proclamation saying that the campaign will begin the following day or week.

2. An appointment is announced. The charity may have appointed a prominent personality to a position of responsibility and this is announced with a further mention of the forthcoming appeal.

3. Speeches referring to matters concerned with the charity are reported.

4. An award is offered. For instance, prizes are presented to schoolchildren or art students for producing the best poster advertising the campaign.

5. An advance exhibition is mounted giving the background

of the work of the charity, with information concerning the proposed use of the money when it is collected.

It is usual to follow up the first piece of news with a stream of further announcements and pictures showing children doing their 'bit' and notable personalities joining in the activities or collecting money for the Cause. When it's all over, amid much ballyhoo, the vast sum of money amassed is announced. Quite often at the bottom of the write-up there is a word or two concerning the next project.

Naturally the big charities rely to a great extent on the individual efforts of well-wishers engaged in activities which have been covered in the previous chapters. I have however made a study of the various special money-making methods used by a number of the large societies and describe some of them below.

Annual subscription
A fixed sum of money is paid each year by members to a society. In return they are kept in touch and notified of its activities and progress. This may include a copy of the society's publication.

Legacies
Many people when making a will include a bequest which will be paid on their death to a chosen charity.

Deeds of covenant
Charitable societies are enabled under the Finance Act to recover tax on subscriptions paid under Deeds of Covenant. The donor covenants to pay a certain amount every year for seven years. Each year he signs a certificate to the effect that he has paid income tax at the standard rate on the sum subscribed. The charity is then able to claim back from the Income Tax authorities a sum equal to the tax paid. At the moment this means about a 40 per cent increase on the actual amount given.

Donations
Of course, all societies are pleased to receive straight gifts of money at any time.

Pledged gift schemes
One member of a society regularly calls on a few friends and neighbours who give a pledged sum of money for the Cause.

Campaigns and appeals
Special fund raising efforts are floated for specific purposes such as helping the victims of floods, earthquakes, and other disasters or for many less dramatic reasons.

Flag days
Street collections are made to sell flags or poppies. House-to-house collections may be made for the same purpose or to deliver small envelopes into which donations may be placed, to be collected a few days later by a voluntary worker.

Collecting boxes
These are issued to members and others interested in collecting money individually and left standing in prominent places, notably on shop counters.

Collecting miscellaneous items
Many articles can be collected, and in bulk are of considerable value. The following are examples,:

Trading stamps, cigarette coupons, etc.
British and foreign postage stamps.
Milk bottle tops.
Newspapers.
Clean discarded woollen garments.
Old sheets and curtains.
Foreign coins.
Old coins.
Broken spectacle frames.
Bent gold pen nibs
Jewellery.
Binoculars.
Cameras, etc.

Co-op number
The Co-operative stores allot a certain number which customers can quote when purchasing goods, so that their dividend can be forwarded to charity.

Unclaimed articles
Some charities may ask swimming pools, shoe repairers, dry cleaners, etc., to give their unclaimed articles to help raise money.

Hunger lunches
Supporters eat rolls, dry bread and cheese or soup, and drink water or coffee in place of their normal lunch as well as giving a donation to the cause.

Celebrity luncheons
A fairly new scheme has 'caught on' in London and other big towns. A number of celebrities are invited to a luncheon and are seated separately amongst the guests at fairly small tables. This makes it possible for those attending to make direct contact with a notable personality.

Charity balls
These are large glittering affairs, studded with Royalty, debutantes and famous personalities of stage and screen.

Film premières, concerts and theatrical presentations of all kinds
These are well known methods of fund raising which have taken place for a long time. As in the case of charity balls, the success of the ventures depend to a large extent on the personalities who are willing to give their services.

Painting exhibitions
Artists sometimes agree to stage an exhibition of their work, allowing a percentage of the sum raised by the sale of the pictures to go to the charity they are supporting.

Football pools
Privately run football pools are another method used by the national charities for raising money.

Christmas cards, calendars and seals
These can be sold by individual members or in special centres before Christmas. The cards are sometimes designed by handicapped members of a particular society. This has become a most popular form of giving to charity as so many people are sickened by the commercialism which has overtaken the festive season.

Gift shops
Shops in all parts of the country are sometimes borrowed for a week and occasionally on a permanent basis. These shops are almost always loaned free of charge for this purpose and all goods are donated by the public.

Giving lessons
Many instructors of swimming, keep fit and dancing (both ballroom and children's) regularly give their time free to teaching these subjects. The fees collected are sent to a charity.

Penny collections
These take many forms and include the following: Pennies-a-week Appeals; miles of pennies; hundredweights of pennies collected on large pairs of scales; towers of pennies built up on the counters of bars.

Rags
A much publicised form of fund raising usually undertaken by students who devise a number of incredible and remarkable stunts. These are sometimes taken too far, when, for instance, a famous personality is kidnapped and held to ransom or washing is pegged along a clothes line, festooned between the pinnacles of King's College, Cambridge.

Discount sales
Certain manufacturers will supply clothing in bulk cheaply for Discount Sales in aid of well-known charities.

In conclusion

Let us now consider the essentials of fund raising. Do we really need to collect extra money in the Welfare State and if it is handed over to a national charity, is it put to the utmost use? Finally, are the sums raised worth the tremendous efforts and demands made upon our time?

We can, of course, see the point in raising money for local ventures, but also on studying the situation we find that without the money raised by voluntary workers for the larger charities, many people would suffer considerable deprivation. The official bodies in this country connected with the Health and Welfare Services are taken up with day-to-day administration and much of the worthwhile progress has been pioneered by voluntary effort.

Concerning the spending of money once it has been raised, we can rest assured. Practically all charities are entered in the Central Register of Charities kept by the Commissioners and their accounts are open to inspection by anybody who wishes to enquire. Much thorough investigation takes place to ensure that every penny of their funds is wisely spent.

What about the attitudes of people who raise funds? At one end of the scale are those who are enthusiastic about their particular charity, the serving of which dominates their lives and gives them great pleasure and emotional satisfaction. On the other hand, there are many who have been 'caught', having been asked to help by their friends when they possibly feel no special urge to do so. If you fall into the latter group and reluctantly agree to support a cause, do make up your mind to work wholeheartedly and above all, determine to make it a pleasure. Decide to be professional and thorough in your attitude and behaviour and so reap the reward of the satisfaction of work well and truly done. Anyway, for most of us living in more fortunate circumstances, there is a natural human desire to assist where the need is apparent.

Everybody knows that fund raising is hard work. Certainly you will need an iron will, tenacity of purpose and devotion to your Cause in order to carry on. Never allow yourself to be discouraged by the occasional disparaging remark. A great many unkind words have been thrown at the 'do-gooders' in the past, but if you are convinced that what you are doing is right and will help somebody somewhere, don't let anything stand in your way.

Resolve to set to work with a fresh heart and inspiration. Be ambitious in your projects and organise, advertise and improvise! You will do better to gather many people around you than to try and do too much on your own. Don't be too shy to ask anybody for financial assistance or practical help. Without being asked people will not often volunteer.

Remember the schools and youth clubs and other youngsters who are brimming over with energy and almost looking for things to do! People, however, like variety and change; so use your imagination to capture the enthusiasm of helpers and inspire them with your vitality. Take them into your confidence and make them feel they are truly participating not only in the execution but also in the planning of the project. In this way you will increase their interest and may get fresh and lively ideas as well. Remain in charge, but give scope to others.

Be willing to learn from your mistakes and discuss with your committee directly after each event, how improvements can be made on another occasion. Keep a notebook of ideas and suggestions while the present function is still fresh in your mind and suggest that each member keep a file of fund raising projects, cut from newspapers and journals. New methods of fund raising crop up all the time and most can be adapted to suit your particular requirements.

Build up goodwill for your Cause by telling others about the work, aims and purposes of your Charity. After the thank-you letters have been written and supporters told of the amount of money raised, try to maintain a friendly relationship with them throughout the year. A complaint from managers of shops that they are ignored by fund raisers between functions is not without justification. Show interest in their life as well as your own and be sympathetic to other good works in your community too.

In conclusion

Finally, to sum up, what is it that makes some events a roaring success and others a dismal failure? I think the answer lies very much deeper than appears on the surface. The vital and obvious ingredients of planning and hard work must certainly be present, but underneath all this there must be something more. What is this elusive yet magical ingredient?

I believe it often stems from one personality who is warm-hearted and generous in every respect and will always find time to help anybody in trouble. Whether it's her next-door neighbour who needs a baby sitter, raising money to save the refugees in Jordan or for preserving the walruses in Alaska, she will be there, helping to the limit of her capabilities. And what happens when she wants support for a venture? Everybody rushes to her aid and gives whatever they can spare. It may be time, energy, talent, patience, ingenuity, genius, technical ability and any other aptitude they may possess. It is this combined effort of giving straight from the heart which is the spirit which moves mountains, crowns projects with phenomenal success and makes this world a better and happier place for everybody in it.

I hope you will have the good fortune to organise your functions in such an atmosphere; if so, your life may take on new direction and purpose. You will help those in need, make a host of friends, broaden your horizon and, most important of all, raise cash and have fun!

Appendix

(The information below is correct at the time of publication.)

Barnum's Carnival Novelties Ltd,
67 Hammersmith Road,
London W14

Swinnertons Ltd,
Union Street,
Walsall,
Staffs

Sell everything required for fêtes, carnivals and all fund raising schemes.

Beauty Counselors of London Ltd,
Beach Road,
Newhaven,
Sussex

Gives demonstrations on skin care and the art of make up in the home.

Bourne and Hollingsworth Ltd.,
Oxford Street,
London W1

Fred Aldous Ltd.,
The Handicraft Centre,
31 Back of Piccadilly,
Manchester 1

Supply ear-ring mounts and sequins.

British Egg Marketing Board,
Wingate House,
93 Shaftesbury Avenue,
London W1

Issues free leaflet on decorating eggs for Easter.

Copelands Linen Ltd,
Dept. 15, Box 95,
19a Grosvenor Road,
Belfast 12

Sells remnant parcels of Irish linen.

H. F. W. Deane and Sons Ltd,
31 Museum Street,
London WC1

Supplies plays on approval (up to six), also *Textbook on Stagecraft* by Susan Richmond, price 5s.

Appendix

Eagle Star Insurance Company,
1, Threadneedle Street,
London EC2

Eagle Star House,
32/34 Mosley Street,
Newcastle upon Tyne

Arrange insurance for public liability and has a special 'Pluvius Weather Insurance'.

EMI Records,
EMI House,
20 Manchester Square,
London W1

Issues a guide to recordings of folk and traditional dances from Great Britain and other countries.

English Country Cheese Council,
National Dairy Centre,
5–7 John Princes Street,
London W1

Issues free leaflet on cheese and wine parties.

Eroica Recording Service,
31 Peel Street,
Eccles,
Manchester

Supplies records of fairground music.

Folk Dance and Song Society,
Cecil Sharpe House,
2 Regents Park Road,
London W1

Sells records, books of instruction and sheet music.

Samuel French,
26 Southampton Street,
London WC2

F. Wardle Taylor and Company,
33 Lancaster Avenue,
Manchester 4

Supply plays and book *Guide to Greasepaint*, price 2s. 6d.

Wallace Heaton Ltd,
127 New Bond Street,
London W1

Photographic Dealers in large towns

Hire old movie films and films of Walt Disney and the Wild West.

Appendix 103

S. V. Leverton and Company,
62 Finsbury Pavement,
London EC2

Midland Stamp Supplies,
5 Barkby Road,
Syston,
Leicestershire

} Buy quantities of sorted Empire and Foreign and British Commemorative stamps both on and off paper. Those off paper command a higher price.

Lewis Foundry Company Ltd,
Pencoed Works,
Bynea,
Llanelli,
Wales

Buys silver foil milk bottle tops.

London Transport Poster Shop,
280 Old Marylebone Road,
London NW1

Sells London Transport Pictorial Posters.

National Council of Social Service,
26 Bedford Square,
London WC1

Supplies booklet *Voluntary Organisations and the Law relating to Lotteries and Gaming* price 3s. plus 6d. postage.

E. Pearce and Sons Ltd,
Acre Wood Way,
Hatfield Road,
St. Albans,
Herts

J. H. Leighton and Company Ltd,
29–37 Hurst Street,
Liverpool 1

} Buy newspapers and journals tied up in separate bundles.

Performing Right Society Ltd,
29 Berners Street,
London W1

Gives permission for live music to be played at public events.

Phillips and Page Ltd,
50 Kensington Church Street,
London W8

Good quality Art Suppliers in most towns

} Sell brass rubbing requisites.

Phonographic Performance Ltd,
62 Oxford Street,
London W1

Gives permission for recorded music to be played at public events.

104 Appendix

The Potato Marketing Board,
50 Hans Crescent,
London SW1

Issues free leaflets on ways in which to cook potatoes.

Keith Prowse Music Publishing Company Ltd,
21 Denmark Street,
London W1

Publishes old time songs, ballads and sketches.

Selfridges Ltd,
Oxford Street,
London W1

Pontefract Brothers Ltd,
Short Street,
Manchester 15

Sell Tri-Chem paints.

Senduswools Ltd,
Raven Works,
Dewsbury Road,
Ossett,
Yorkshire

Buys old knitted woollens and old cottons, flannelette sheets, pillowcases, tablecovers, etc.

Index

Admission charges, 28–9, 32, 34, 35, 36, 52, 83
Advertising, 7–9, 15, 16, 39, 44, 53, 55, 59, 72, 87, 93
All the Fun of the Fair, 24–5
American shower gift stall, 26
Annual subscriptions, 94
Antiques, 41
Aprons
 gingham, 26
 paper, 82
Art of Barbecue and Outdoor Cookery, The: the Tested Recipe Institute, 47
Astrological diversion, 34–5

Baby show, 87–8
Balloons, 24, 30, 88, 89
Banners, 21, 75
Barbecue, 47
Barbecue and Beat night, 44
Bargain box, 49
Barnums Ltd., 16, 21, 24, 31, 33, 35, 59, 84, 89, 90
Barrel-organ, 20
Bath puff, 79–81
Bathroom stall, 49
Bazaars, 21–2, 23, 26–7, 61
Beach bonfire party, 37
'Beating the Bounds', 39
Beauty contest, 87
Beauty Counselors of London, 36
Beauty demonstration, 35–6
Beer and Skittles evening, 28
Bicycle
 polo match, 44
 racing, 19, 68
Blow outs, 24
Bon Marché fête, 18–19
Bookmarkers, 75–6
Books, 55, 66, 71
Bottle kicking and Pie scramble, 51
Bowling, 24
Bowling for the pig, 83
Bows and Arrows, 26

B.P. Book of Festivals and Events in Britain: Christopher Trent, 25
Bran tubs, 20
Brass rubbings, 81
Bric-a-brac, 23, 41
Bridge drive, 33–4
'Bring and Buy' sale, 32, 38
British Egg Marketing Board, 51
British Music Hall, The: Mander, 31
British Red Cross, 1, 16
Brunch party, A, 42–3
Bucket ball, 67, 84

Cabaret, 19, 33
Cake stall, 23, 72
Caledonian Market, 23–4
Calendars, 60
Campaigns and appeals, 95
Cancer Research, 1
Candles
 lighting the, 85
 snuffing the, 66, 85
Cardboard cut-outs, 21, 24, 53, 56–7, 58
Card Fortune Telling: C. Thorpe, 35
Cards
 Christmas, 59
 fortune telling, 35
 valentine, 30
Carnival, A, 43–5
Carol singing, 65–6
Catch a Fish, 66, 87
Catering, 6, 16, 28, 34
Celebrities, 8–10, 39, 44, 46, 53, 87
 approach to, 11–12
Celebrity lunches, 96
Central Register of Charities, 98
Chamber of Horrors, 24, 67
Charities Digest, The, 2
Charity balls, 96
Cheese and Wine Parties, 36
Cheese and Wine party, 29, 36
Cheshire Homes, 2

106 Index

Children
  care of, 20
  and fund raising, 62–9
Children's gift stall, 59
China and glass, 23, 42, 50
China smashing, 84
Christmas
  cards, 59, 97
  crackers, 78–9
  festivals, 48, 56
  grotto, 58
  tree decorations, 59
  table centre, 77–8
Citizens' Advice Bureau, 2, 91
Climbing frame, 20
Cloakroom facilities, 7
Clowns, 92
Coconut shies, 24
Coffee morning, 7, 31–2, 33, 70
Collections of
  goods, 12, 50 ,71, 95
  money, 39–40, 46, 63, 65, 70, 94–5
Collectors' Corner, 71
College of Further Education, 71
Comedy Rugby Match, 45
Commercial help, sources of, 8, 12, 20, 35, 36, 42, 46–7, 50, 51, 52–3, 54, 55, 58, 72, 84, 85, 87, 99
Committees, 5–6, 12, 32, 34, 35, 44
Competitions, 23, 24–5, 26, 27, 48, 51, 52, 54, 68, 84–9
Conjurers, 92
Continental Bazaar, 26–7
Co-op numbers, 96
Copelands Linen Ltd., 22
Costumes, 19, 21, 23, 25, 26, 27, 31, 33, 34, 35, 40, 46, 52, 64
Costumes for School Plays: Barbara Snook, 31, 64
Cover the silver pieces, 66, 86
Crepe paper, 20, 29, 30, 45, 59
Crockery, 23, 50, 73

Dances, 28, 30, 34
Dancing, 27, 29, 63, 65
  children's, 91
  folk, 21–2, 91
  Highland, 25, 30, 91
  Morris, 25, 48, 91
  national, 91
  square, 34, 46
  traditional, 25
Darts, 18, 42, 66, 85
Dates for Functions, 7

Deane, W. H. and Son, 64
Deeds of covenant, 94
Display, 72–3
Dog show, 88
Do-it-yourself exhibitions, 53
Dominoes, 42
Donations, 94
Dressing up stall, 67
Drinking milk from a baby's bottle, 88
Ducking for apples, 29

Eagle Star Insurance Company, 15, 17
Easter
  festivals, 48, 52
  frolic, 51
Egg and Spoon race, 67
Egg cosies, 26
Electric bell ringer, 86
E.M.I. Records, 22
English Country Cheese Council, The, 36
Eroica Recording Service, 16
Exhibitions, 53, 92, 96

Fashion shows
  champagne, 52
  spring, 32, 48
  tots to teens, 64–5; *see also* Mannequin parade, millinery parade
Festive food stalls, 59
Fêtes, 7, 18–19, 24, 25, 26, 83–91
Films, 19, 20, 21, 24, 26, 27, 55, 92, 93, 96
Flag days, 95
Flags, 21, 26, 27
Floats, 44–5
Flower
  arrangements, 32, 51
  arrangements Societies, 49, 51, 53
  festivals, 48
  pot contest, 68
Folk Dance and Song Society, 34, 46
Food and Information Centres, 20
Football pools, 96
Fortune telling, 35
Fried chips, 90
Friends of the Hospital, 1, 29
Fund raising
  purpose of, 98
  attitude to, 98–100

Garden produce stall, 23, 50, 71, 72

Index 107

Gay Paree, A night in, 33
Gift
  stall, 72
  shops, 97
Giving lessons, 97
Goldfish in bowls, 24
Golf championship, 37
'Good as New' stall, 71
Grand Carnival ball, 45
'Guess the Lucky Egg', 51
Guide to Greasepaint: Samuel French, 31, 64
Gymkhana, 37

Hallow-e'en party, 29
Halsbury's Law of England, 14
Handbook of Old Irish Dress, McClintock, 22
Handicrafts, 54, 73
  stall, 72
Hat and Hair style parade, 51–2
Helpers, 2, 5, 18, 20, 21, 28, 33, 39, 46, 54, 70, 83, 99; *see also* Children, and Commercial help, sources of
Herbs and Spices: R. Hemphill, 50
Herbs stall, 23, 50
History of Ireland: Chauvire, 22
Hobbies fair, 54
Holiday Memories, 55
Hoop-la, 24
  laundry, 85
Hot Pot supper, 28
House and Garden gala, 49–50
How to Play Roulette, Chemin de Fer, Baccarat and Blackjack: Morris Hughes, 33
Hunger lunches, 96

Insurances, 15–17, 37, 44
Irish Cookbook, My: Monica Sheridan, 22
Irish Folk Tales: Curtin, 22
Irish Tourist Board, 21

Jazz Bonanza, 45
Jewellery, 23, 72, 77
Jokes and tricks, 24, 26
Judo, 24, 91
Jumble, 9, 23, 27, 48, 67, 71

Keith Prowse Music Publishing Company, 31, 64
Knobbliest knees, 24, 88

Knock off the Hat, 66, 86–7

'Lassooing the Steer', 26
Legacies, 94
Libraries, use of, 20, 22, 31, 32, 45, 68, 91
Licensing laws, 14
Lighting, 28, 29, 58, 67
Local Yokels programme, 44
Lollipop
  fair, 62, 66
  races, 67
London Transport Poster Shop, The, 23
Lucky numbers, 44

Madeira morning, A, 38–9
Mad Hatters' Ball, 52
Magazine stall, 55
Magicians, 91
Making Posters: Vernon Mills, 9
Mannequin parades, 53, 64–5, 92
Marbles, 42
  championship, 51
Market stall, 41
Marquees, 16
May Day Miscellany, 48
Maypole, 25
Mentally Handicapped Association, 41
Merchandise, procuring of, 12–13, 20, 22, 23, 71
Michaelmas mart and hobbies fair, 53
Mid-summer revel, 48
Millinery parade, 92
'Missile Search, The', 35
Most elaborate hair-do, 88
Most glamorous grandmother, 88
Most shapely ankles, 44, 88
Music, 19, 23, 24, 26, 30–1, 53, 63–4, 65
  copyright fees for, 30
  fairground, 16
  live, 14–15, 33, 91
  recorded, 15, 22, 25, 27, 34, 39, 59, 67
Musical evenings, 54

National Council of Social Service, The, 14
National Stalls, 18, 26
New Year's Eve dance, 30
'Nosh up' stall, 66

108 Index

Objets d'art, 23, 71
Obstacle race, 68
Old Tyme Music Hall, 30
Orange rolling, 51
'Over Sixties' club, 38
Oxfam, 2, 93

Paint, 21
  Tri-Chem tubes, 74
Pantomimes, 63
Paper wavers, 24
Paperweights, 77
Parties, 29, 36, 40–1, 42
'Penny on the Square', 83
Performing Rights Society, The, 14, 15
Phonographic Performance Ltd., 15
Physical Education and Sport, 91
Physical Education Training Centre, 24, 90
Piggyback race, 68
Pin cushion, 76–7
Places for functions, 7
Planning, 5–6, 19, 70, 93–4
Plays, copyright of, 15
Pledged gift schemes, 95
Pluvius Weather Insurance, 17
Pneumatic drill, 90
Police, 39, 44
  regulations, 13
Pomanders, 74
Pony
  clubs, 35, 37
  rides, 90
Portrait sketches, 91
Posters, 8–9, 18, 19, 23, 24, 27, 39, 87
Potato Marketing Board, 22
Pram race, 45
Prams, best decorated, 88
Premises for functions, 7, 16, 18, 28, 33, 34, 35, 36, 53, 55, 58
Press, 7, 8, 23, 33, 91, 93
Prices, 28–9, 34, 36, 38, 39, 41, 44, 56, 89, 90
Printing, 8–9
Prizes, 34, 35, 44, 52, 67, 84–9
  procuring of, 12–13
Programmes, 9, 44
Progressive Party, *see* Safari party
Publicity, 6, 8–9, 33, 39, 44
Public address system, 16
Punch and Judy Show, 24, 92
Punch party, 29
Puppet show, 68, 92

Queen of the May beauty competition, 48
Quoit tennis tournament, 42–3

Raffles, 14, 29, 31, 34, 36, 38, 39, 43, 53, 54, 66, 72, 84
Rags, 97
Records, 23, 71
Relay races, 68
Rick rattles, 24
Ringing the bottle, 85
Roaring Twenties dance, 28
Roll-a-penny, 24
Roundabouts, 20
Round Tablers, The, 20

Sack racing, 20–1, 68
Safari party, 40
St. Andrew's Day dance, 30
St. David's Day dance, 29
St. John's Ambulance Brigade, 16, 39
St. Patrick's Day bazaar, 21–2
Sausage sizzle square dance, 34
Save the Children Fund, 93
Scatter cushions, 26
Seedlings, 50
Seeds, 70
See-saws, 20
Sherry
  morning, 71
  party, 39
Shove ha'penny, 42
Sideshows, 18–19, 20, 24, 42, 66, 83–4
Skittles, 42, 85
Socials, 28–36
Spastics Society, 2, 29, 93
Speakers, 32, 35, 55–6, 62
Sponsored walks, 39–40
Stars and Stripes bazaar, 26
Statues, 68
Stomp and Sheep Roast, 46
Strawberries and Cream Tea, 37–8
Sundowner party, 39
Swimming pool, 18
Swings, 20

Table tennis tournament, 43
Talents project, 70
Teacup Fortune telling: Minetta, 35
Tennis tournament, 37
Textbook on Stagecraft: Susan Richmond, 31, 64
Theatricals, 28, 30–1, 44–5, 64
Three-legged race, 67

Titles and Forms of Address, A Guide to their Correct Use, 10
Toffee apples, 24
Tombola, 36, 43, 54, 59, 72, 89
Tots to teens fashion show, 62, 64–5
Tourist offices, 20, 21, 27
Toy fair, 56
Toys, 20–1, 23, 26, 58, 59, 66
Traditional events, 21, 25, 51
Traffic
  control and direction of, 15, 39
  parking facilities, 7
Trampoline, 24, 90
Tramps' supper, 34
Transport, 28, 39, 41, 47
Treasure hunts, 35, 41–2, 84

Unclaimed articles, 96
Useful addresses, 101–4

Valentine dance, 30
Victorian Music Hall Entertainment, 39
Voluntary Organisations and the Law relating to Lotteries and Gaming, 14

Wallace Heaton, 24, 36
Warblers, 24
Water festival, 37
Watch stopping competition, 88–9
Water tournament, 44
Watney Book of Pub Games, The: Timothy Finn, 42
Weight lifting, 24, 91
What Your Hands Reveal: J. Sheridan, 35
Wheelbarrow race, 68
Whist drives, 28
White elephants, 23, 41, 66, 71
Window dressing: G. Faziakerley, 72
Women's Institutes, 16, 83
Wooden spoons, 81–2

Ye Olde Englishe Fayre, 25
Youth Clubs, 1, 16, 99
Youth Club Skits and Stunts: Sid Hedges, 64
Yuletide bonanza bazaar, 59

Zoo, 24